IMAGES
of America

BAY AREA
ROLLER DERBY

Roller Derby's "Ponytail Express," Barbara Mateer of the Los Angeles Braves duels the Bay Bombers' Carol "Peanuts" Meyer, No. 32, while Capt. Annis "Big Red" Jensen, No. 38, and Judy Sowinski, No. 33, keep an eye on the situation during a sellout 1959 game at the San Francisco Cow Palace. One year before, the Derby was moribund, but Jerry Seltzer, son of founder Leo Seltzer, got the Bombers on KTVU television and turned the game into a thriving enterprise all over the country. Mateer and Jensen skated well into the 1960s, Meyer was a Bomber mainstay until the game folded, and Sowinski was training skaters in the new women's game right up to her passing in 2011. (Courtesy of Les Pulkas.)

ON THE COVER: From left to right, the Southern Eagles' Sandra Dorenberg tries to outrace the Bombers' Barbara Baker, No. 38, and Pauline Kaderya, No. 39, in 1972. (Courtesy of Phil Berrier.)

IMAGES
of America

BAY AREA
ROLLER DERBY

Jerry Seltzer and Keith Coppage

ARCADIA
PUBLISHING

Copyright © 2012 by Jerry Seltzer and Keith Coppage
ISBN 978-1-5316-6310-0

Published by Arcadia Publishing
Charleston, South Carolina

Library of Congress Control Number: 2011941627

For all general information, please contact Arcadia Publishing:
Telephone 843-853-2070
Fax 843-853-0044
E-mail sales@arcadiapublishing.com
For customer service and orders:
Toll-Free 1-888-313-2665

Visit us on the Internet at www.arcadiapublishing.com

This book is dedicated to all the people who helped make the original Roller Derby what it was and to the people who are making today's Roller Derby what it is and will be!

CONTENTS

Acknowledgments		6
Introduction		7
1.	Beyond the Marathon	11
2.	Bay Area Derby	19
3.	Go, Bombers, Go	29
4.	Big Red and the One and Only	67
5.	Mister Roller Derby	73
6.	The Golden Girl	83
7.	Thrills and Spills	87
8.	Beyond the Bombers	115

ACKNOWLEDGMENTS

In all its incarnations, Roller Derby is about teamwork. Our thanks go to the supreme fans of the original game for help in finding, and sometimes identifying, skaters and situations: Gary Powers, Phil Berrier, Mark Roman, and Joe Peters. Special thanks go to Les Pulkas for assistance with the rarest 1960s material. From the track, all-star skaters John Hall, Gloria Mack, Cliff Butler, Carol "Peanuts" Meyer, Loretta "Little Iodine" Behrens, and No. 40 himself, Charlie O'Connell, filled in the blanks, which was no easy task. The Rollergirls came through in the contemporary sport, with special thanks to the "Lipstick Librarian" (they do not give their "street" names) for putting me in touch with so many great ladies of the new game who shared their thoughts and their pride. Unless otherwise noted, all images are courtesy of the authors.

INTRODUCTION

Roller Derby founder Leo Seltzer had worked for Universal Pictures in the 1920s, starting at the age of 17, eventually opening three of his own movie theaters in Portland. Moving east, he became a promoter of the era's walkathons and other attractions at the mammoth Chicago Coliseum. He sought to distance his events from the rather tawdry aspects of the 'thon attractions of the day, and his contestants were well-scrubbed, personable young people who, while desiring to win money and other prizes, played to the fans who paid their 10¢ for some entertainment during the dreary days of the Depression. Reading in a magazine that the vast majority of Americans had been on skates at one time or another in the course of their lives, a spectator sport on skates seemed like a surefire enterprise for Leo's promotional skills.

The skaters in that first race in Chicago, beginning on August 13, 1935, were reflective of the times, skating endlessly in a marathon to win at least a few hundred dollars but getting meals and lodging, reason alone during the Depression to join up. Even then, being involved was a little on the subversive side, and portentous of things to come, not everything was as it appeared to be. In fact, the winning team in that first race was composed of a boy, just 16, who had lied about his age and that of his female partner.

Cots were stationed in the huge infield for contestants to rest until it was time for them to get back on the track again. Breaks in action prompted them to do entertainment routines with the audience throwing coins in support. Dancing, singing, stunts, and musical performances were some of the skills on display. A skater needed to be a good vaudevillian, also a sign of the game's future. This showmanship was in addition to the requirement that the skaters, 25 coed teams of two, would alternate with each other to skate nearly 12 hours a day, with every player having to log a certain number of distance miles. Amazingly, in light of today's short attention spans, Chicagoans ambled in to watch an event that began every day at 1:30 p.m. and ended at 12:30 a.m.

The bouts of today's Bay Area Roller Girls were known as races then and were strictly endurance based. In those early days, a skater had to compete from New York to Los Angeles as little lights shone on a huge US map to indicate a player's progress, illuminating their supposed arrivals in Pittsburgh or St. Louis. Winning skaters notched nearly 3,000 miles in the Transcontinental Roller Derby. In the initial race, Clarice Martin and Bernie McKay, the wily 16-year-old, came in first on September 22, 1935, after having started the race on August 13, more than a month before. Indeed, the partners were so hardy a duo that they held the lead from September 11 on and never relinquished it. The twosome left the attraction after being accorded their title and the stunning $1,000 cash prize, with second and third place contestants netting $500 and $250, respectively.

With modifications, Seltzer took his event on the road around the country, spending weeks at a time in various cities. Ivy King, a champion speed skater considered the first star of the Roller Derby, was a bespectacled crowd pleaser. But it was a full year before the first bright lights of the race developed, including heartthrob Wes Aaronson who, when the troupe moved to Los Angeles, was linked with trilling film star Jeanette Macdonald and Josephine Bogash, nicknamed "Ma" because she was 39 years old at the time, ancient in the athletic world of the day. She and her young son Billy were always crowd favorites; on more than one occasion, Bogash would bawl out or start a shoving match against anyone causing any kind of injury to her son. Seltzer provided all materials (food, sleeping arrangements, regular health checkups, and showers) to players free of charge.

It was not the skating alone that drew crowds back for another session, but also the skaters themselves. Some newspaper columnists correctly referred to the skating event as a program, but others described it, even superlatively, with a term all skaters then and now would come to hate: "show."

Television was nowhere to be found in the 1930s, and Seltzer had to gamble on some cities where the Roller Derby flamed out quickly. Even in these uncertain years, sketchy rules evolved in which designated "jammers" would break out of the circling pack of skaters, catch up to the rear of the pack, and attempt to pass members of the opposing team for points, a basic plan that remains in place to this day.

By the time the skaters made their first appearance at San Francisco's Civic Auditorium in 1938, the flat track had given way to an intimidating banked structure, which allowed for entertaining stunts and propelled skaters in and out of turns at breakneck speeds.

A friend of Seltzer's made a fateful contribution to the game in the late 1930s. Writer Damon Runyon, remembered chiefly for his vintage baseball stories and the warmhearted characterizations of New York street dandies that became the basis for movies like *The Big Street* and the musical *Guys and Dolls*, convinced Seltzer to incorporate body contact. Thus, the rocking/socking aspect of Roller Derby enjoyed and vilified by observers became a part of the game.

Rules seemed lost on 1930s audiences, who cheered loudly if someone outpaced someone else, if someone fell, and if anyone engaged in fisticuffs, which began to occur more often. Ironically, today's audiences at mostly female bouts often also seem happy just to be let in on the action, with only the vaguest idea of how points are scored. This concerned Seltzer greatly.

Selzer and company had to campaign hard for media coverage. "Think you've seen everything? You're wrong!" trumpeted the headline on the *San Francisco Chronicle* sports page when the Roller Derby opened on July 5, 1938. The game's debut in the Bay Area was quite an affair. Mayor Angelo Rossi fired the starting gun, with coeds from University of California, Berkeley, and Stanford on hand to give the game some youthful gloss. Bathing beauties, ubiquitous in the era, added additional cheesecake appeal. In one promotion, sassy Gracie Freid competed in a match race against Billy Bogash. Sexism viewed as gallantry prevailed as Bogash awarded her a half-lap head start one night and a quarter lap the next. She won the first one, dropped the second, and demanded a rematch on the grounds that Bogash pushed her. An enthralled *San Francisco Chronicle* writer informed readers that 10,000 fans in attendance would testify that he did no such thing. Both teams erupted into a total brawl, the police arrived, the fans became swept up in the hysteria, and in the melee, Gracie Freid, "the most hated of the girl skaters," was apparently "knocked out colder than December 22 in Minnesota." And, most importantly from the standpoint of the Roller Derby, the *San Francisco Chronicle* writer predicted things would only get hotter as the series progressed. In his duty as a reporter, he did everything but provide a phone number for ticket reservations.

For another trip, Seltzer minimized travel expenses by taking his troupe across the still-new Bay Bridge for a new home in downtown Oakland's cavernous Ice Arena. It was here, in August 1938, that the game drew such big crowds night after night, and the Roller Derby returned many times in the years to follow.

Seltzer resented the zanier aspects of a typical race, observing with consternation that skaters responded to the crowd in ways more apropos of show people than athletes. He was, however, a realist. Throughout its history, advertisements for the Roller Derby were placed alongside movie listings in newspapers, only rarely in the sports section. Also, Seltzer's informal research indicated that women drew the audiences and men kept them returning.

"One grand melee," a writer described an evening at the Roller Derby in Oakland, involving elements of "football, fighting, wrestling, speed and endurance skating, and the constant noise of a thousand workers drilling rivets into the steel ribs of a ten story madhouse." Though the Ice Arena was sold out night after night, as soon as Roller Derby left town after its initial run, there seemed to be a sigh of relief from the sporting crowd. Writers were alluding to a somewhat sad question of the Derby fan's life that, if at some point one did not believe in the attraction, what good was it? With total legitimacy, 21st-century skating has rendered this question obsolete. But in 1939, reacting to the Derby's missing Oakland on its next go-round, a columnist snarled that this was "the best news of the year."

Staggering through World War II and all the problems that came with it, the Derby had a single touring unit of two teams barnstorming the country. (In the best of times, two or three units would be in play.) A race with women only was attempted in desperate wartimes. After a couple more races, the game was absent in the Bay Area from 1942 until 1949, when it went on ABC television and became an overnight sensation. On the West Coast, fuzzy films (coast-to-coast television was not readily available at this point) of games in New York made everyone a fan as ABC broadcast first one night, then a second, then a third each week of New York Roller Derby, all year long. Returning to Northern California, "Your Ford Dealer in the Bay Area," actually some 60-odd dealers in nine Bay Area counties during the postwar auto boom, sponsored a ladies' night in January 1950 with ABC's KGO-TV in San Francisco. All a lady need do was call up the box office, mention the name of her local Ford dealer, and she would have a free ticket with payment of the 25¢ federal tax, of course. All games were played at the Oakland Auditorium, a sturdy, small arena that was old even in 1950 but would become the Bay Bombers' favorite venue a decade later.

Rolling into a heavy cash infusion, the skaters had long since moved out of the arenas they were playing in and had began to rent their own apartments or stay in residential hotels, since at this point the game did not stray too far from the city a team would call home. For the rest of its existence, Roller Derby would field no more than six teams in any given season, it being somewhat risky for the Seltzer family to carry the more than 100 skaters in their National Roller Derby League.

Serving Oakland were the California Westerners. When they played a stand at, say, Seattle, they became the Seattle Westerners. The stars of the early 1950s became iconic in Roller Derby lore; they seemed to never retire. The Chiefs' Gerry Murray was the most famous female skater, bar none, her closest rival being Midge "Toughie" Brashun, the Derby's bad girl. Stars emerging in the Bay Area included Tommy and Buddy Atkinson, two superb skating talents in the sport almost from the beginning; Ann Calvello, who got her start in a short-lived, imitation Derby outfit; and Jean Porter, invariably referred to as "Jeannie Porter, the Indian Girl," who posed for photographs with the requisite feather sticking up from her hairdo. Porter was considered quite lovely, and her somewhat shy personality endeared her to Derby audiences, so much so, that not long after the games began airing on ABC she was signed to do a pseudo-documentary for Paramount called *Roller Derby Girl*. The one-reel film was typical of the day, when all movie theaters played "shorts" along with cartoons and previews prior to the main feature. It was actually a fairly realistic (if melodramatic) behind-the-scenes look at what it was like for a girl to join the Roller Derby, complete with Midge Brashun as the "you're-never-gonna-make-it-kid" voice of experience.

The beloved "Ma" Bogash was still skating from time to time. Carl "Moose" Payne was a hero for Jolter fans, along with his wife, Monta Jean. Away from the glaring eye of skater matrons from their days of living together as a unit, some skaters did court and marry. Buddy Atkinson married Bobbie Johnstone, a crowd-pleasing talent from the early days. Russ "Rosie" Baker wed, appropriately enough, Annis "Big Red" Jensen. The marriage of the tempestuous Midge Brashun to young Ken Monte was less publicized; he was not yet in his 20s and Brashun was five years his senior, something akin to scandal in those days.

Roller Derby, constantly on television, began to be somewhat annoying to some. Promoting the game, getting new talent ready as older skaters left, lodging, salaries, logistics of touring, television, and production were beginning to take a toll on Leo Seltzer. Contract hassles led Seltzer and ABC not to renew their agreement in 1951. Seltzer felt, correctly, that there were simply too many games being broadcast every week, but, to his shock, no other network rushed in to carry the Roller Derby.

The saga of the Derby's rise and fall on television illustrated that very often, once something is a television hit, that is what it will be forever. A mortal blow, after cancellation audiences plummeted from thousands to hundreds. Seltzer spent a fortune on newspaper advertisements and radio spots, but Roller Derby was dead in New York. The 1953 playoffs had been held in Madison Square Garden; just one year later, the biggest night of the year for the game was celebrated in the hoary Fourteenth Street Armory. The following year, tiring of the business and also taking on new real estate interests, he eventually relocated his family, with skaters in tow, to California—the one place that had never let him down.

One

Beyond the Marathon

"You see," Leo Seltzer said in 1935, "nearly every man, woman, and child has skated, or tried to skate, on rollers. But thus far, there never has been an outlet for champion roller skaters, I mean, a national outlet. Everyone knows about roller skaters, but there are no champions, no standards, nothing for the enthusiastic roller skaters to shoot at. We are remedying that."

> LEO. A. SELTZER'S
> Trans-Continental
> ROLLER DERBY
> OR
> COAST TO COAST ROLLER SKATING RACE
> (NAME REG. IN U. S. PAT. OFF. 1935-1937 BY LEO A. SELTZER)
>
> JANUARY - FEBRUARY
> 1939
> MUNICIPAL AUDITORIUM
> Memphis, Tenn.
>
> Open Nightly - 7 to 11 P.M.
>
> FIVE CENTS PER COPY

Ice sitting was one of the many diversions during Leo Seltzer walkathons in Chicago. Others included seat-side singers, musicians, jugglers, comics, ventriloquists, fire-eaters, and more. These kinds of one-joke mini-attractions were everywhere in the arenas that Seltzer's attractions played, and some crept into the Roller Derby at first.

An American dreamer, Montana-born businessman Leo Seltzer (1903–1978) created one of the only sporting events not derived from something else. Always wanting the game to be something more than entertainment, he saw no reason why the Roller Derby could not someday succeed in the Olympics.

Another crowd packed in for Seltzer's penultimate event before presenting the Roller Derby, "The Race of Nations." This was "Amateur Night" at the Chicago Coliseum, though there were rarely any professional walkers at a Seltzer walkathon.

Hollywood cutup Fifi D'Orsay was a friend of Leo Seltzer. Seen as something of a scandalous bad girl, the actress played the image onstage and in films and made appearances at Seltzer's shows to liven up the proceedings. His insistence on family entertainment ensured she would not be too outré for the coliseum.

For many years following its debut, Roller Derby looked for local sponsors for individual skaters and teams. Sportswriters fawned over the young man whose tattoo of a woman was scraped off his hip, a deaf skater who taught his female partner to communicate with her hands, and the young lady named Hoover who was supposedly a cousin of the president. From left to right are Gordon Cleveland, Roy Gowin, Ted Randall, and Tom Whitney in 1939.

Bert Wall (center), racing two unidentified players at a rink, was an enduring Derby star in the 1950s. Initially, Roller Derby tried to be chummy with roller rinks (or "flat tracks" as they are referred to by skaters) and held several events and promotions at local skating palaces. Very quickly, these rinks turned up their noses at the supposedly uncouth and vulgar Derby personnel.

15

During one of the earliest Bay Area appearances, Russ "Rosie" Baker (center), so named because of his chubby (and rosy) cheeks, engages in fisticuffs with a skater while unidentified referees try to intervene. Baker would go on to marry teammate Annis "Big Red" Jensen, and the Bakers became the first leaders of the Bay Bombers in 1954, even recruiting their daughter Barbara for the team in 1968.

LEO A. SELTZER
Originator and Managing Director, Transcontinental Roller Derby.

FOR VICTORY
BUY
UNITED STATES
WAR
BONDS
AND
STAMPS

"A Roller Derby League in Every Section of the Country"

As it stands today, the Roller Derby is fast becoming the realization of a "dream come true". When the sport first originated, Leo Seltzer's goal of creating a Roller Derby league in every section of the country was only a dream. Right now it is an actual fact.

A Roller Derby Team consists of five boys and five girls, and is known by the name of its home city—i.e.—the "New York Gardens Team"; "Chicago Cardinals", "Detroit Olympians", etc. Two teams engage in a "meet", which includes from twenty one to twenty eight "games", each night's skating constituting one game. During the three hours skating nightly, the girl skaters alternate with the boys at fifteen minute intervals. Points are scored by the individual skaters who must lap the field within a two minute period, passing a skater of the opposing team to gain a point.

Twice each night five minute "open house" periods are staged, the most exciting portion of the Roller Derby's entertainment. It is a race in which all skaters participate, and it is possible for one team to gain from one to five points through sheer speed. Pictured above is a typical Roller Derby crowd. So enthusiastic are average Mr. and Mrs. America about the sport that they fill the largest auditoriums in FOUR of the country's largest cities EVERY NIGHT!

ROLLER DERBY ASSOCIATES
23 E. JACKSON BLVD. CHICAGO, ILL.

Seltzer proudly predicted a future where every major city would have a Roller Derby team. World War II prevented this, and at its conclusion, the Derby had to start virtually from scratch. The photograph in this promotional advertisement is the only surviving image from the first Roller Derby race on August 13, 1935. In many ways, Seltzer's vision is now true, as Roller Derby teams are in scores of cities all over the country and the world.

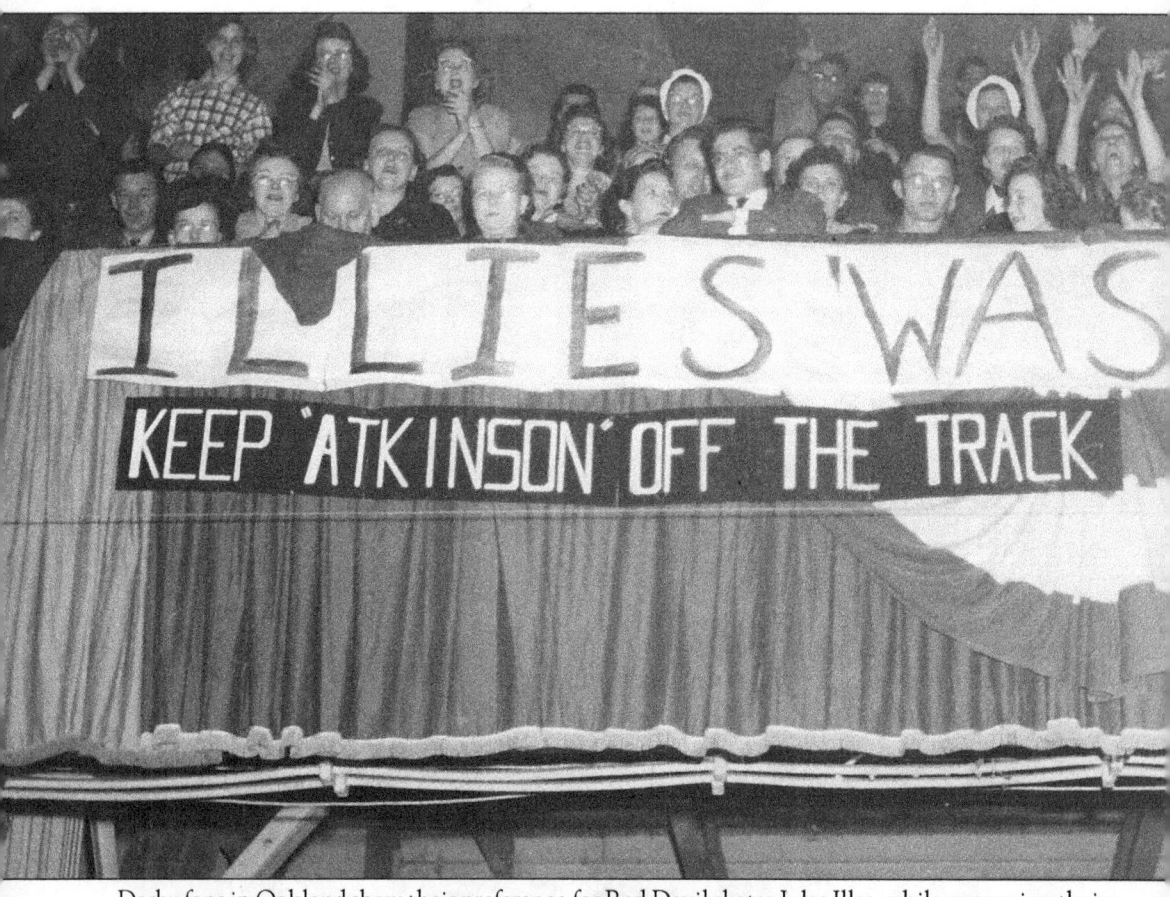

Derby fans in Oakland show their preference for Red Devil skater Jules Illes, while expressing their fervent hope that Buddy Atkinson will remain out of the way. Though Atkinson was injured at the time, his presence was felt on the track at inopportune and downright illegal times. Oakland quickly became a regular stop for the Roller Derby.

Two
Bay Area Derby

Seltzer sent units out from Chicago whenever business dictated. This late-1940s appearance shows the track far higher than in later years; however, purists in the 21st-century game have been wistfully calling for a return to high banks. To the right of the track is the giant jam clock that would count down the two-minute heats. In Bay Area games, a then trendy, digital countdown clock was often used in the 1970s.

Three Bo's and a Peep were the credited session singers who turned a little ditty about the game "Where You See Everyone Having Barrels of Fun, What a Thrill!" into a minor hit. Composer Leonard Whitcup was a friend of Seltzer's from Chicago who penned a lot of songs and music for Westerns of the 1930s. Diehards sing the numbing chorus—"They go 'round and 'round and 'round at the Roller Derbeeee"—endlessly.

Buddy Atkinson chats up his biggest fan, daughter Julie, sitting beside his wife, Bobbi Johnsone, in Oakland in 1950. The skating Atkinson clan—Buddy, wife Bobbie, brother Tommy, son Buddy Jr., daughter-in-law Dru Scott, grandson Sean, and granddaughter Ali—is the first family of Roller Derby. Today, Buddy Jr. works with roller girl groups and is a consultant for track construction.

Gloria Mack (left) and her husband, Billy Gardner, were one of the most popular skating couples. Here, she is unfazed by San Francisco's Ann Calvello as she simultaneously blocks out Joan Kazmerski (rear) in 1954. "Those were the days . . . so much fun!" she says. Today, she corresponds with fans and skaters on Facebook. (Courtesy of Gloria Gardner.)

Teri Anderson laces up in San Francisco in the early 1950s. The Roller Derby Skate Company supplied team skates, and every Roller Derby television series incarnation promoted them heavily. But by the 1960s, the skate of choice for Derby personnel was from a rival, the Chicago Skate Company, specifically for its maneuverable Jet model.

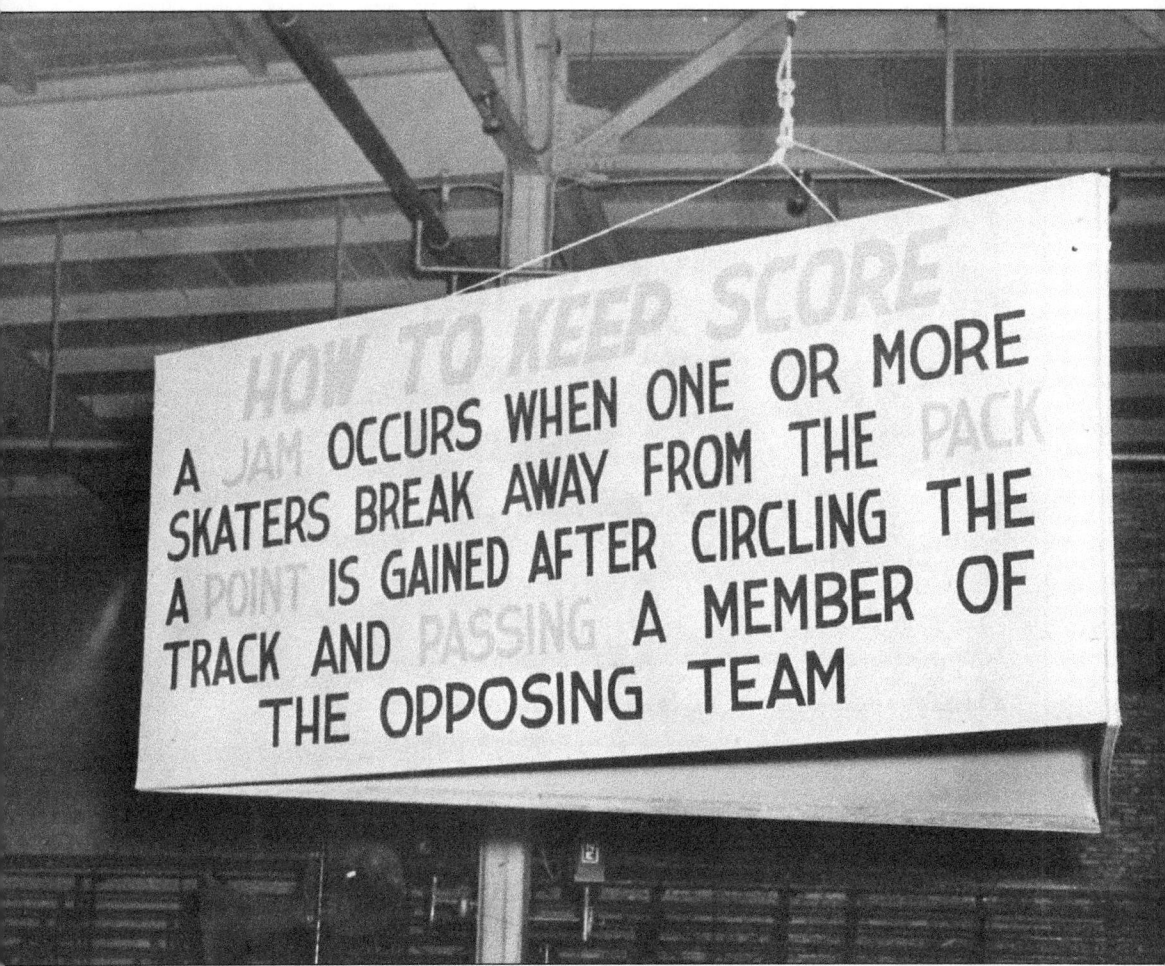

Here, the rules are explained to Oakland audiences in 1949. The simple rules: designated skaters called "jammers" lap members of the opposing team. The rules have never really changed in seven decades and are employed by today's mostly female leagues. The audience, then as now, is not always clear on the specifics of the rules.

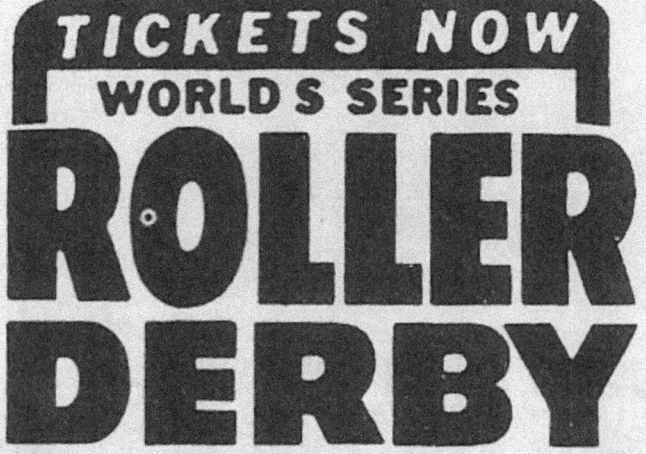

New York audiences had a lot of entertainment choices in the summer of 1951, with the Derby flying high thanks to television. By the fall, though, the game was off the air and headed for devastating problems. Ironically, in 1973, after the Shea Stadium playoffs in New York, the Derby was again on its way to ruin, this time, it seemed, for good.

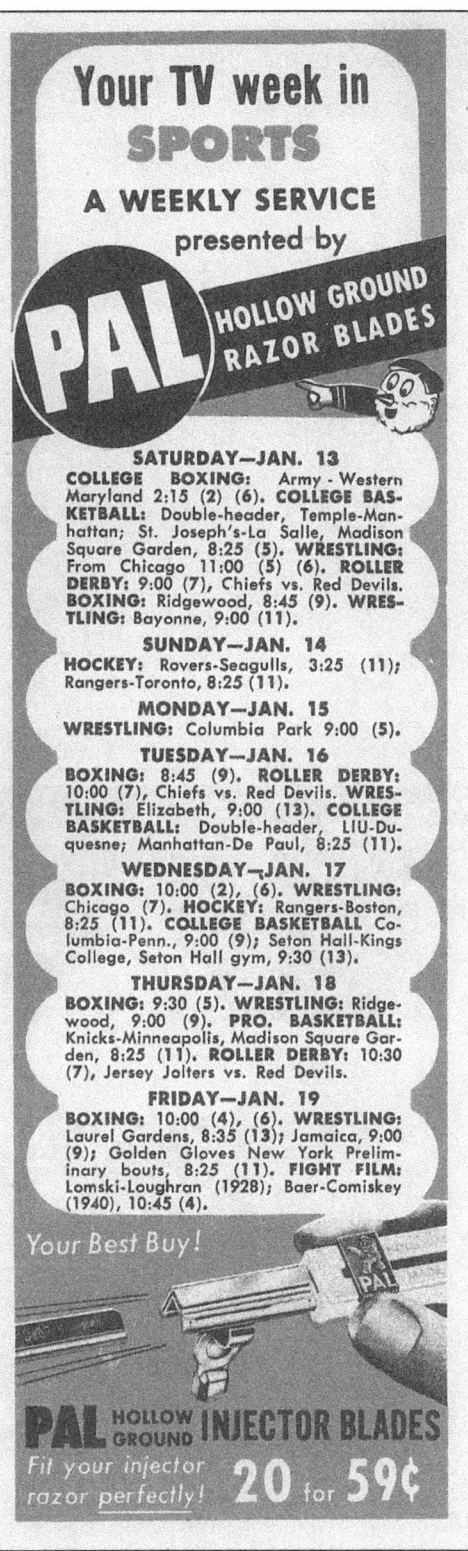

Roller Derby was constantly on prime-time television beginning in 1949. In its earliest days, ABC depended on Roller Derby for big ratings and got them. Seltzer was concerned about overexposure and wanted to curtail some of the broadcasts, but ABC held him to a contract that gave them the right to broadcast the game as much as they wanted, with disastrous results.

```
WESTERN UNION
W. P. MARSHALL, PRESIDENT

Paid                 Roller Derby Associates           3:00 pm

                                                November 29, 1951

Mr. Fred Morelli
Coliseum
1513 S. Wabash Ave.
Chicago, Illinois

        NECESSARY ADVANCE $5000 SKATERS TOMORROW TO MEET THEIR
        SATURDAY PAYROLL. THIS IS MINIMUM TO KEEP THINGS TOGETHER.
        WRITING LETTER REGARDING OTHER MATTERS. REGARDS.

                                                Leo Seltzer
LS:sa
```

Seltzer authorizes funds from the reserves to pay the skaters. Without television, the box office dried up. Skaters were sometimes paid late, but, according to tradition, they got paid first. Sadly, the recipient of the telegram, Fred Morelli, unsuccessfully sued Roller Derby in 1972 for a chunk of the fading business. Defending the suit made the game's dubious financial health even more uncertain.

In the friendlier atmosphere of Oakland in 1952, Buddy Atkinson is not so injured that he is unable to hustle his New York Chiefs into action. He would be running around the infield coaching, hassling, and cajoling teams and fans for the next 20 years and training new talent for the Bombers and other teams in the Bay Area.

Elmer "Elbows" Anderson, No. 31, keeps an eye on current Bomber Tommy Atkinson in 1958. Elmer had been with the game since the 1930s; here, he is in an old-timers' exhibition tilt in Oakland. Tommy, one of the Bombers' early coaches, was killed in a car crash shortly after this game. His nephew Buddy Jr. would lead the Bombers briefly in 1971. This photograph is somewhat symbolic of the major change happening at the time. Leo Seltzer, giving up hope that the game would amount to much in successive years, turned the enterprise over completely to the care of his son Jerry, who would, with the proper promotional zeal, not only rescue the family business, but cause it to thrive as never before in the 1960s.

| HARRY CHESSER | JOE CANEVARI | PHIL KADUBEC | JOE FOSTER | EDDIE AHERN | GERRY RAPP | BILL REYNOLDS | AL STEWART |
| ANN CALVELLO | MIFFIE MIFSUD | ANNIS JENSEN | MARY GARDNER | BEVERLY WALLACE | TONI LOOMIS | GYPSY STONE | |

BAY BOMBERS   **ROLLER DERE**

Early Bomber teams were often comprised of whoever wanted to travel to San Francisco from Los Angeles, where the Derby was based in the mid-1950s; iconic names familiar to many longtime fans often populated the team. "Wild" Bill Reynolds (second row, right) was coach. Phil Kadubec, (second row, third from left) was a source of fascination to the media; he was concurrently a psychology major at the University of California, Berkeley.

Three
GO, BOMBERS, GO

Bombers
Gloria Mifsud, Carol Jacobs, Annis Jensen, Connie Bernal, Hillary Bennett, Margo Senninger
Chuck Piper, Eddie Ahern, Dick McDowell, Lou Guzman, Russ Baker, Johnny Casar, Bob Brown, Bob Josef

Proudly wearing their Golden Gate Bridge jerseys, the first official Bay Bombers are ready to roll in 1954. "Big Red" Jensen led a team of mostly unknowns, while "Rosie" Baker's men's team was slightly more experienced.

Joan "Joanie" Weston passed herself off as a novice at her early-1950s training sessions at the Rose Bowl, when in fact she and a girlfriend used to sneak into the unlocked venue where Weston would take her first turns around the track during the game's off-hours, arousing suspicion upon her entry into the league four days after she attended her first training class. The male-dominated sporting world of the time offered few career paths for young women like Weston, who became a fan watching the game on television and knew instantly that this world was for her.

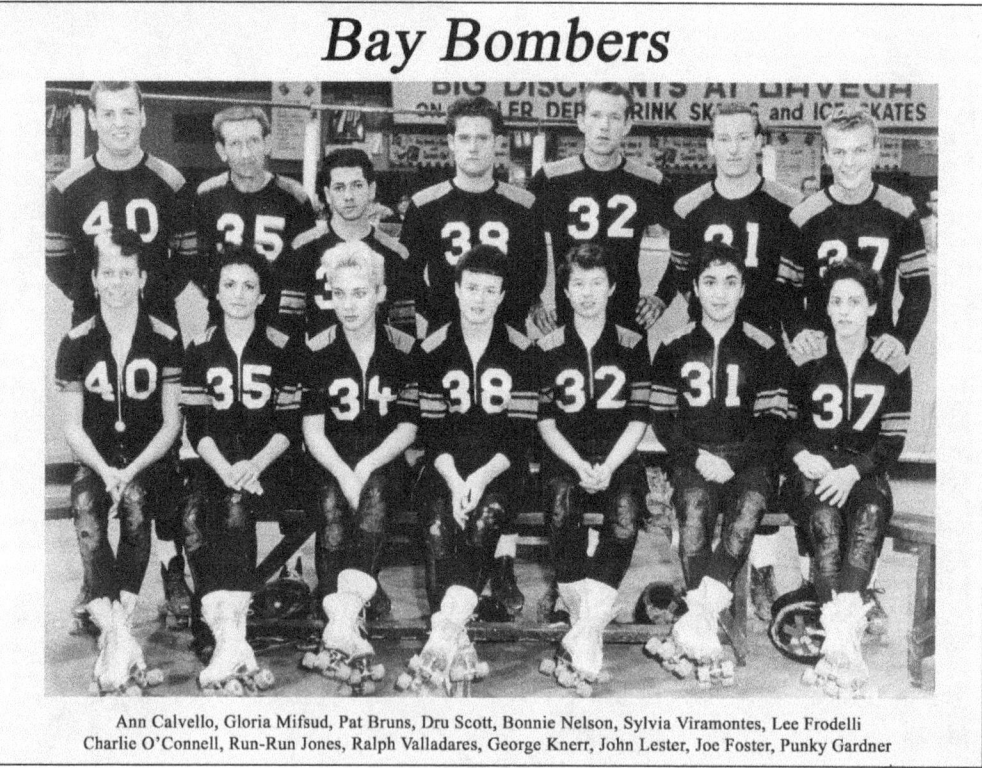

Bay Bombers

Ann Calvello, Gloria Mifsud, Pat Bruns, Dru Scott, Bonnie Nelson, Sylvia Viramontes, Lee Frodelli
Charlie O'Connell, Run-Run Jones, Ralph Valladares, George Knerr, John Lester, Joe Foster, Punky Gardner

The Bombers are pictured here in San Mateo in the late 1950s. Ann Calvello, No. 40 (first row, far left), was women's captain in the absence of pal Annis Jensen, injured at the time. Her on- and off-track partner was young Charlie O'Connell, or "Charlie O," No. 40 (second row, far left). The game was still considered somewhat "in" from about 1958 to 1960 in the Bay Area, so much so that the tumultuous romance between the two skaters was fodder for gossip columns. Readers wrote in to ask of their wedding plans.

Each week, Walt Harris welcomed television audiences to "the last half of another exciting Roller Derby game," between the San Francisco Bay Area Bombers and some lesser club. He would highlight the Bombers, led by Annis "Big Red" Jensen and Charlie O'Connell, along with shining talent like scoring aces Frankie Macedo, Joe Foster, "Wild Man" Bobby Seever, and Judy Sowinksi. Joe Foster holds the record for most points scored in a game; Carol "Peanuts" Meyer, No. 32, became one of the most beloved skaters of all time.

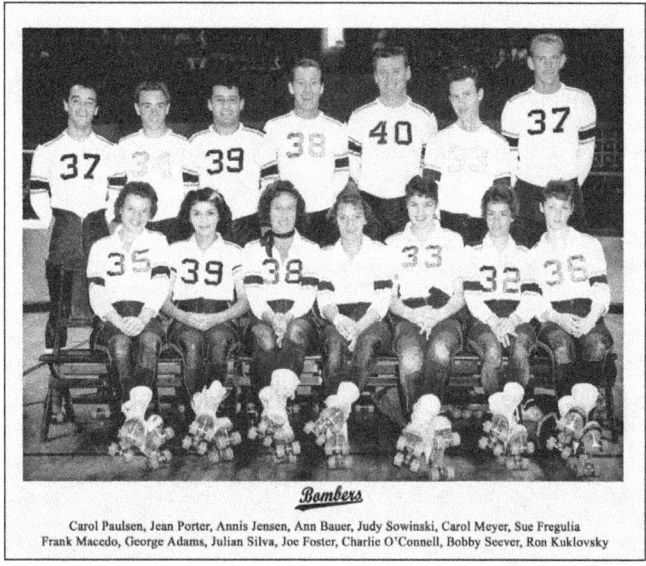

Bombers
Carol Paulsen, Jean Porter, Annis Jensen, Ann Bauer, Judy Sowinski, Carol Meyer, Sue Fregulia
Frank Macedo, George Adams, Julian Silva, Joe Foster, Charlie O'Connell, Bobby Seever, Ron Kuklovsky

Bombers
Terry Hooper, Pat Wallace, Carol Meyer, Annis Jensen, Barbara Mateer, Judy Sowinski, Robin Bridges
Charlie O'Connell, George Adams, Randy Akin, Ron Kuklovsky, Bert Wall, Lou Donovan

The Bombers early-1960s space-age uniforms are pictured here. Walt Harris would bring the television audience up to speed with the following, for example: "O'Connell and Bert Wall, going at it all night," "Jensen and Gerry Murray going at it all night," "All tied up after a wild first half," "O'Connell making good on his promise to . . ." and beckoning them with, "The girls are at the starting line. Let's get down on the track and pick up the action!" Millions of viewers were ready to watch.

California Bombers

The early-1960s Bombers needed a regular home. A low-rent wrestling outfit had a hold on the city-run Oakland Auditorium, and Bomber fans took offense. A practical mother penned, "I know wrestling has been here since 1932, and that's nice, but children aren't interested, and let's face it times change." Would it not be better, she wrote the city council plaintively, "to have boys and girls at the Roller Derby and not out somewhere roaming the streets?"

Pictured here are Leo Seltzer's stars of the 1940s and 1950s, Jean Porter (she was called the "Indian Girl" in less-enlightened times) and Gerry Murray, the game's female star in Oakland. Murray's career was more oriented toward New York operations, but she came to the aid of the Bombers in the late 1950s and early 1960s before leaving Roller Derby completely and skating for other outfits that surfaced through the years.

Either Walt Harris, on television, or the public-address announcer would stop mid-sentence and proclaim the start of the most hysteria-inducing tactic in all of Roller Derby: "A pull-away by the Bombers!" In a pull-away, one team literally ran away from the other, who chased them with abandon while the crowd went wild. Bombers girls "Big Red" Jensen, Pat Wallace, "Peanuts" Meyer, and Bobbie Mateer escape their early 1960s oppressors at the Cow Palace.

OAKLAND BOMBERS

Indoors or outdoors in 1959, the Oakland Bombers reigned supreme. In a roster packed with rough fan favorites (at O'Connell's insistence) were Ralph Valladres, No. 34, who was a sensational jammer and Fletcher Saunders, No. 36, who was one of the earliest African American skaters (Bomber or otherwise) and a real fan favorite. "Big Red" Jensen, No. 34, and Ann Calvello, No. 40, were so beloved on the girls' squad that it mattered little who they skated with.

Promotions were Jerry Seltzer's game, and the Derby was full of fun and creative ones. At Berkeley's Ice Arena, "Peanuts" and Dewitt Quarles, winners of a Derby twist contest, are an interracial dancing couple in 1962, a time when it could not be done on television's *American Bandstand*. Other promotions: games played on an aircraft carrier and a horse racetrack as well as events like a skateboard match race, "skate-offs" with one or two periods of a previously disputed game re-skated, a mini-game series between football's Raiders and 49ers, and more!

The Braves' George Copeland (right) gives an elbow to an unidentified Bomber in Oakland in 1962. Copeland was one of the first African American skaters in the game. Bay Area skating audiences in particular seemed color blind, and fans of color supported their Bay Bombers and loathed their opponents no matter who they were.

More than one skater has worn a football helmet to protect an injured (or broken) nose or chin. Annis Jensen wore one several times, here in 1962 (left) assisting Anne Bauer, No. 40, in trying to contain Los Angeles favorite Margie Laszlo in a Richmond game.

The Brooklyn Red Devils' Gail Fund defends against Cathie Read in San Jose. Initially, Jerry Seltzer and his nominal publicity people insisted the game was real. The biggest fallacy believed of the Derby is that the outcomes of the individual games were predetermined. By and large, they were not. Seltzer trusted his skaters implicitly to know what was needed in a situation, what was working promotionally, and always with an eye on the future.

The Chiefs and Bombers are pictured here in Richmond in 1962. The 1973 rules stipulate that when a pack is formed, each team has a pivot skater (black helmets) up front, two blockers (solid colored helmets) in the middle, and two jammers (striped helmets) in back. After forming, the whistle blows and the jammers must work their way past the blockers and pivots to break out of the pack, catch up with the rear of the pack, and for every member of the opposing team they pass, they receive one point in a one minute jam.

The Bombers pull their man over the Braves for points in 1961 at Berkeley's Ice Arena. Blockers could not hold hands, but they could lock wrists and arms.

The Grand Slam in Roller Derby is five points, indicating all skaters on the other team have been passed. Typically, if a visiting skater scored the grand slam, he or she would throw up a triumphant hand with five fingers extended in order to taunt the hometown crowd. Here, the Braves' Bobbie Mateer needles the Bomber fans at the Cow Palace in San Francisco in 1962.

The Bomber girls take a time out to huddle during a playoff game at the Cow Palace, listening to Annis Jensen for directions. Friendships among skaters, as any Derby participant will assert, have always been the heart of the game. "It was always, kind of, us against the world," Bomber Tony Roman once explained. Present-day women skaters find that skating garners lasting bonds.

The Bomber boys take their own break at the Cow Palace. In the Derby's original incarnation, it was always assumed that the girls kept the game from being accepted as a sport but also were the ones who drew a large audience into the arenas. It took a long time for Bomber star Charlie O'Connell to accept this, and he generally paid little attention to the women's race, as it was called.

To a skater, a hand for a whip is important, but what is most important to Roller Derby are the strategically placed phone numbers, always visible on the penalty box in full view of the cameras videotaping this and hundreds of other games at Kezar Pavilion in San Francisco. Long before computer ticketing, operators were standing by to take phone reservations. Pictured here are the Braves in 1961.

Buddy Atkinson Jr. (left) was one of only a handful of skaters to wear glasses on the track. Superbly gifted and long thought of as a skater of equal (or greater) ability than Charlie O'Connell (right), Atkinson spent most of his career with the Chiefs and never quite became a first-tier rival to O'Connell. He left for another organization to become a star skater but returned to the Bay Area, thrilling fans as the coach of the Bombers in 1971.

Buddy Atkinson Jr. (center) takes his turn wearing a football helmet in 1961 in San Francisco. On the right, scooting past the conflict is Mike Gammon, considered the greatest jammer in the history of the game.

Mike Gammon, No. 25, readies for action on the New York Chiefs as the men take over the game from the women. Gammon's mother is Gerry Murray and his father was skating star Paul Milane. He rolled for the Bombers briefly at home but often on the team's cross-country tours. Behind him, also No. 25, is his then wife Judi McGuire.

Children run freely in downtown Oakland, streaming toward an early-1960s Bomber game at Youell Field, the initial home of the Oakland Raiders. Skaters never particularly liked outdoor games in the Bay Area because the nights would often get chilly, and dew in the evening would make the track extra slippery. Youell was demolished in 1969 to make way for a Laney College parking lot.

Dewitt Quarles (right) of the Bombers battles the man who would become the team's favorite jammer in a few years, Tony Roman, in San Francisco. Almost annually, there would be a large piece in one of the major Bay Area daily papers addressing what they saw as the grim reality of Roller Derby's popularity, which had eclipsed every major sporting event in the Bay Area in terms of viewership and attendance, except the Giants. Each piece, some condescending, some aghast, centered on the roughness, the obvious contrivance of the game, and the fact that the fans believed, apparently, every second of it. Often in the same issue, and sometimes on the same page near the bottom, would be a two-paragraph write-up on the previous night's game.

Roller Derby fans have always been able to walk right up to the track and talk to skaters, sometimes in the middle of the game. Usually, a security guard will escort them back to their seats. Here in San Francisco, a fan addresses the Los Angeles Braves. She may have been objecting to some "color," a Derby term meaning theatrical conflicts, personalities, and/or fisticuffs.

Bedlam breaks out at Kezar Pavilion as fans storm the track. Kezar, basically a basketball gymnasium, was the perfect size for a game, but fans would often stampede the track and lean in under the rails to watch any kind of fracas, terrifying the skaters. It often happened during television tapings, which gave the impression that the game was really something to see in person.

George Adams (left) suffers at the arm of George Copeland in San Francisco in 1959 before a packed house. When Bay Area newspapers, the *San Francisco Chronicle* and the *Oakland Tribune*, printed up box score summaries and small write-ups with misspelled names and scoring errors filed by game announcers, Derby people and fans took the time to call them in to the late-night sports desk. Enthusiastic Bomber Boosters saw no reason why there should not be more coverage. They were never given the true reason: the papers hated the Derby and thought it was a complete show.

The jammer in front could put an end to a jam by placing the hands on the hips, a practice that continues in most leagues to this day. Just who is in front on a banked track is sometimes at the hairline judge of a referee. Three referees on the infield were ideal in the original game: one would watch the home team for points and penalties, one the visitors, and the third everything in between.

Bob "Woody" Woodbury restrains a Bomber in San Jose . . . illegally. Races between Woody and Charlie O'Connell would spike attendance regardless of where the game was skated. This was especially true in 1968 and thereafter. When Charlie O'Connell retired, Woody was chosen to replace him on the Bombers, but O'Connell missed skating and returned to the track within weeks. There was no room for Woody, and an obvious rivalry developed when he was dispatched to the New England Braves. Their match races caused attendance to soar to such a degree that, through the years, they would even race each other on occasion when the Bombers were playing a team other than Woody's. Years later, O'Connell characterized Woody as "a lovely man, a really good guy. Not much of a skater, but just a fine human being," sentiments that would shock audiences of the 1960s had they discovered that this was one bitter rivalry all for "color."

Looking like extras in a James Dean movie, skaters relax at halftime out of fans' sight in this rare photograph showing inter-team fraternization. For outdoor games in Antioch, Vallejo, and any number of Bay Area communities with fairgrounds, players drove right up to the track in their cars in uniform. At game's end, still in uniform, players sped off into the night to a local motel where Jerry Seltzer would rent a few rooms for changing and showering.

A match at Kezar Pavilion in San Francisco draws a typical packed house in the early 1960s. Built in the 1920s, it was home to more Derby games than at any other location in the Bay Area. The skaters liked the small arena, and across the street the fabled Kezar Club (now Kezar Pub), a sports bar, was a favorite after-game hangout. The no-frills venue is bleachers-only, and even a few hundred fans packed in sets up a fearful din. The Bay Area Derby Girls skated a doubleheader there in 2011.

Margie Laszlo, screaming at Kezar, was a Bay Area Roller Derby favorite her entire career. Her brief stint as a print model in the Los Angeles area made good copy for Derby yearbooks ("Once a model, now a terror"). Heavily influenced not only in skating style by Barbara Mateer, Laszlo wore her hair long enough to be pulled and yelled and shrieked in protest if things did not go her way. In the early days of the Bombers, she was a roommate of Joan Weston, with whom she developed a fierce track rivalry. Rarely the captain in league competition, she was always the star of any girls' squad. She essentially took over Weston's role on the Bombers in 1972, in fact, only becoming the Bombers cocaptain (with "Peanuts" Meyer) in the final season of the original Roller Derby. Her long hair, shrieking exclamations on track, and gracious behavior with fans made her a valued friend and foe of Weston, Calvello, and other skaters, and Bay Area followers held her close to their hearts as the one girl they wished was a Bomber.

Here are three of Roller Derby's finest. From left to right are Margie Laszlo, Annis Jensen, and Barbara Mateer in action at Kezar Pavilion, where hundreds of Bomber games were taped and shown all over the country, making the noisy, sweltering, little gymnasium one of the most famous and beloved in all of American sports.

"Dynamite" Mike Gammon (left), the "Fastest Man on Skates," tries to scoot past Joe Foster in 1961. Not much of a "red shirt" (visiting team) skater, Gammon dazzled all Derby fans with his amazing speed and agility and is considered a virtually peerless skater.

Match races were rarely held at Kezar later in the game's run, but in the early 1960s they were fairly frequent. Here, Charlie O'Connell, in the middle of everything again, tries to hold his ground against other skaters from various teams.

The Bombers' Anne Bauer, No. 40, tries to score against Ann Calvello, No. 2, in an early-1960s Cow Palace game, while Annis Jensen, No. 38, and an unidentified skater roll nearby. To be a Bomber girl skater, though every Roller Derby aspirant dreamed of it, was sometimes perceived as the kiss of death by skaters themselves. Only a handful achieved star status. What marriages there were, later in the game's history, often occurred on the team. Anne Bauer married Gil Orozco, Charlie O'Connell's backup through the years, a man the Bay Area fans accorded special affection and dignity for his quiet, proud service to the Bombers.

Carol "Peanuts" Meyer, right, rolls against the Hawaiians' Betty Peterson, No. 76, at Kezar. "Peanuts" is wearing the gang's Captain Marvel uniform. The Bomber skater was, after Annis Jensen and Joan Weston, easily the most popular Bomber female ever.

Charlie O'Connell, right, in his space-age Bomber jersey, races John "Porky" Parker at Kezar. Stately Joan Weston is wearing the satiny jacket of the New York Chiefs in the background. Flying around the track as they were, the boys' hair did not move, slicked at the time with pomade, somewhat popularized in the game by O'Connell years after it was in style. It gave the Bomber men a kind of retro, tough-guy look.

The Bomber women, with Judy Sowinski (far right) leading the way, throw a pull-away maneuver at Richmond Auditorium in 1961.

The Chiefs' Judi McGuire (center) was a Bay Area favorite, even though most often on visiting teams. She and her husband, Mike Gammon, were almost always the top scorers for the league in any season.

Certain Bay Area locations were so important the Bombers had individual contracts with them for a certain number of dates each season, a practice that continued to the end of the original game. Richmond Auditorium was one of the best venues for the Bombers. Today, Richmond has its own team, the Wrecking Bells, who skate regularly a few blocks away.

It would be unthinkable for an audience member even to touch an athlete today, but in Roller Derby, close interaction was, while not encouraged, tolerated, especially if fans were helping out. Today's Roller Girl audiences are similarly so close to the action that they too often retrieve flying helmets and hoist up fallen skaters.

"Peanuts" Meyer stands over a fallen Bomber teammate, seen clutching her lower back. "Peanuts" was merely 4 foot 11 inches, one of the smallest skaters around. When a skater would take a bad fall, there was always concern, with other skaters hovering around them to make sure they were all right. A physical therapist or trainer would often be on the infield to help out. Injuries (most often to wrists and arms), were frequent, yet surprisingly few career-ending mishaps occurred in the game, simply because no skater wanted to quit for any reason. They skated with broken limbs and noses and all manner of other injuries to stay in the game. Unwritten rules dictated that competitors avoid hitting those sensitive areas.

Judy Sowinski, No. 33, defends against an unidentified jammer at the Cow Palace. Relatively new to the game at the time, her salary was about $100 a week, plus $25 for food on the road. A medical courier after retiring, she was a revered coach at age 71 for the Penn Jersey Devils female team based around Philadelphia in the 21st century.

"Peanuts" Meyer (left) rolls against the Hawaiians' Dolores Doss at Kezar. The Bombers had several San Franciscans on the team but the Hawaiians fielded few Islanders.

The Roller Derby Skate Company's Street King model was the first outdoor shoe skate for children and the top of Jerry Seltzer's line when he was a mere salesman for the company. The skate outlasted the original game, with a photograph of Kezar skating action gracing the box for years to come.

Before the game, Charlie O'Connell, No. 40, chats with his players. Later in the 1960s, as befitting his reign, he could not be bothered with warm-ups, preferring to make a grand entrance during the first period, upstaging the girls' race.

Charlie O'Connell, center, horses around with his teammates during warm-ups. The behavior of the early Bomber men was boyish and fun, and interplay like this charmed fans at live games.

The Westerners' Mary "Pocahontas" Youpelle (right) and Anne Bauer maneuver around the curves in 1964. Liquid on the track (perhaps a Coke hurled by an angry fan) resulted in powder being thrown down. The well-liked Youpelle was actually Italian, married to teammate Red Smartt. The veteran couple was a fan favorite for many seasons.

Gil Orozco (left) was with the Bombers for almost his entire career. A handful of Bomber men became stars but almost never became coaches on rival clubs because Charlie O'Connell wanted them on his team. Lou Donovan had a reckless skating style and was particularly popular in his native San Francisco. "Cowboy" Dave Battersby was seen by some as talented enough to have his own team. George "Run-Run" Jones was another Bay Area favorite. Some Bomber men started on the ultimate career path when O'Connell employed them at his cocktail lounges in Alameda and San Leandro. Sturdy Julian Silva was a star jammer throughout the 1960s, while frantic Bobby Seever learned his craft so well that he became a second-string rival of O'Connell when he left the Bombers in the mid-1960s. New Yorker Joe Canaveri had an aggressive style O'Connell favored. Hefty Pete Boyd, the "Moving Wall," had a formidable blocking presence. Dewitt Quarles was a star jammer and was a Bay Area crowd-pleaser in the 1960s.

This is the "push off," or changeover, between periods. A tradition since the 1930s, the exiting women's team would circle the track one more time, the men would join them, and the ladies would give a nudge to their male counterparts as they rolled off the track; the men repeated the procedure at the end of their periods. With as many as 30 skaters on the track at the same moment, it was a somewhat tricky demonstration of skill, and more than once a trip or collision took whole teams down to the floor. But the hardest aspect of the changeover is to maintain a steady, unspectacular pace in sync with everyone else. Television tapings prevented this time-consuming activity, and it fell into disuse in the 1970s, or on occasions when, Ann Calvello noted, "We were too damn tired. It takes a lot of work out there!"

Annis Jensen (left), always a fierce competitor, and Judy Sowinski, No. 33, double-team an unlucky Westerner in Santa Cruz. Fans loved the move, unless it was performed on a Bomber.

In a match race, Ken Monte lowers the boom at Kezar Pavilion. The jump block was one of the toughest to execute properly. Monte was considered a tough coach. "He would hit and kick his own skaters, but I sure learned quickly," his protégé Cliff Butler says with a laugh.

Gerri Abbatello (left) tries to score for the Cardinals against Annis Jensen in Richmond in 1964. She and her husband, skater Joe Chaump, produced a skating son for the game in later years.

Annis "Big Red" Jensen played for a team called The Redheads during World War II and as the tallest was nicknamed Big Red." Here, she delights in blocking out an unidentified skater at the Cow Palace.

Four

BIG RED AND THE ONE AND ONLY

In the new game that started in the 21st century, everyone in the Roller Derby is important. But the original Derby was built on stars, usually three per squad: the coach or captain ("top skater" in Derby jargon), a key backup skater ("second skater"), and a top jammer. The Bombers' first real star skater was Annis Jensen, a holdover from the game's early days. Though she ran a tight ship, she was a motherly skater and fine trainer. Girls sometimes complained Jensen did everything on the team, and the opportunities for others to shine were limited, but she wanted to know it was done right. Smiling and always friendly to fans to the end of her career, she was fine with her bizarre (for the 1960s) job. "I feel I actually have a better arrangement than the average working wife and mother," she once remarked. When it became time to have different leadership in the evolving game of the 1960s, it was not a happy time for Bomber fans. Still, Jensen remained a beloved figure and one of the most popular skaters in the game, skating for visiting teams and smiling for pictures for her loyal followers.

Annis Jensen (left) and Anne Bauer, No. 40, cannot quite contain Margie Laszlo (far right) in Oakland. Jensen wore the football helmet a number of times in her career. "You learn to skate with a lot of pain; you just have to take care out there," she once said.

Ann Calvello, No. 40, was a media favorite in San Francisco and showed up in a lot of sports and city gossip columns before newspapers began an effort to ignore Roller Derby's growing popularity. In the 21st century, she befriended roller girls who wrote and visited her, encouraging her young fans to keep at their craft.

After her calamitous romance with Charlie O'Connell ended, Ann Calvello asked to be traded to another team. She landed on the Braves and enjoyed sparring with her old teammates like Annis Jensen (above). She ended up being the game's premier visiting female skater, enraging the fans that once adored her. Below, she clearly is having a good time with Anne Bauer (left) and Judy Sowinski (right) in Oakland. Calvello in particular was fond of Jensen and insisted younger skaters give her the respect she felt she deserved. The two reunited as teammates several times. Whenever fans would praise Calvello with compliments, she would remind them she was not alone out there and chide them not to forget Gerry Murray, Annis Jensen, and others, even archrival Joan Weston. Skating "red," she would tell people, was much more fun.

Whether on the home or visiting team, Calvello was not hard to spot. She wore contrasting colored gloves (usually her team colors), rolled up (or cut off) sleeves, a swinging religious necklace, and a helmet with her name stenciled across it. Opposing skaters would note that they not only had to watch out for her blocks, but also for her necklace, known to smack skaters in the face at breakneck speed. When the senior Annis Jensen retired in 1969, Calvello became the oldest skater competing and, by extension, the oldest woman on any professional sports team, an honor she relished, often comparing herself to George Blanda of the Raiders, a kicker considered an oddity when he was playing in his 40s.

Garish lipstick was part of Ann Calvello's appearance, startling in the early 1960s. Here, she duels her friendly foe Annis Jensen in a 1963 battle. Calvello, Jensen, Ken Monte, and Charlie O'Connell were all in the Derby Hall of Fame. They were honored when they retired, or gave indication that they might be shortly. Some others in the Derby Hall of Fame, Jerry Seltzer suggests, were honored to "get the hint" that it was time to quit. Not having the heart to cut anyone outright, his custom for dealing with talent that had seen its day was simply not to invite him or her back for the next season. Younger skaters were not always wild about being on Calvello's teams. Jensen in particular heard a lot of complaints about her but brushed them away with a smile. "She's as good as gold," Joan Weston agreed. "If it's good for Roller Derby, she'll do it." As a visiting skater, she attracted venomous fans like few others. For a time, she was considered Roller Derby's second female star. For their part, Jensen and her husband, Russ Baker, made a unique contribution to the team they founded—their daughter Barbara Baker became a Derby fan favorite her rookie season in 1968.

Two of the most honored and talented skaters in the men's game square off. Mike Gammon (left) was rarely a coach, but after a lifetime in Roller Derby, he was the acknowledged leader of several teams without the official title, often the actual coach or captain bowing to his leadership. In the early 1960s, Charlie O'Connell (right) was the game's outstanding star, receiving considerable admiration from a reluctant press. His noncommunicative off-track demeanor assured him privacy, so few writers tried to get to know him. These two skaters had no real rivalry, but Gammon's stature and ability was such that he was one of the few men O'Connell would seemingly allow to get the better of him. In a quirky postscript, after their skating days were over, each man ended up marrying the other's ex-wife; Gammon wed the virtually unknown skater Vicky Cooper, and O'Connell wed star talent Judi McGuire.

Five
MISTER ROLLER DERBY

Charlie O'Connell became the star of the team long before he became its coach. Even as a young star, he was able to play the game either legitimately or otherwise, and many skaters assert that O'Connell was, along with rival Ken Monte, the most dreaded of all skaters; little of what these men did was for show.

Initially, under the guidance of Bomber coaches like "Wild Bill" Reynolds, Charlie O'Connell (right), with Bob Hein, took little direction from any designated leader. Instead, he became the star of the game almost from the beginning via KTVU, Walt Harris noting what a crowd-pleaser he was, and a spectacularly gifted skater. Over six feet tall, Charlie looked the part of the Bomber hero, too, more popular than any of the women or the team itself.

Charlie O'Connell (right) casts a contemptuous look at his biggest rival, Ken Monte of the Red Devils. Monte was his favorite opponent, followed by Freddie Noa, who did not transition into the late-1960s game. Developed in 1960, the new-look position game favored O'Connell, as it would all team stars, as it placed them in the front of the action, often dooming mid-range talent to the center of the pack, where no one could see them.

Charlie O'Connell and Ken Monte are at the starting line for a match race. Since it was not technically a sport, but rather an attraction, everything revolved around Charlie O'Connell. Jerry Seltzer found him "surly, and he wanted to be left alone. Scowling constantly, but what a great skater. He rarely would do interviews unless on our telecasts, and that only added to his persona."

Charlie O'Connell and Ken Monte head toward the finish line. The sensationally gifted Buddy Atkinson Jr. and other top male personalities seemed to be kept at a distance from first-tier stardom by O'Connell, the sole, bankable personality of the game beginning in 1960.

Bob Hein, a secondary rival to Charlie O'Connell, takes him on in the early 1960s. Hein eventually joined the Bombers and had a lot of conflict with O'Connell, real or contrived, that startled Bay Area fans in 1970. When O'Connell finally left the team, Hein was its nominal coach.

Charlie O'Connell takes on the Chiefs' Dave Pound, a major defenseman in the early 1960s.

Few athletes are considered definitive in their sport; mention the original Roller Derby and chances are it will be superstar "Charlie O" who will be the first name on anyone's lips. Ken Monte (left), racing O'Connell in a match at Kezar, was his best foe; their teams were similarly constructed of tough guys. Ken Monte coached and did some officiating but kept coming out of retirement to skate again.

Today, fans think of Charlie O'Connell as the premier defenseman, but until the 1964 season, he regularly jammed several times a game. Here, he chases Mike Gammon during a 1962 jam at Kezar Pavilion. As the Derby progressed, the speed of the game slowed down and the pivot skater, not the jammer, was the main point of interest.

Charlie O'Connell, No. 40, takes on several opponents at a fairgrounds game. Later in his career, he would take nights off and not visit the smaller communities; "out with an injury" would be the explanation. His fellow skaters would shrug, "That's Charlie," meaning he got to do what he wanted. O'Connell's rivals sometimes resented what seemed to them as total capitulation to his wishes.

Chiefs' skaters stand at a dueling flattops race at Kezar Pavilion. When a coach or team captain was in a match race, players were expected to stand no matter what the situation. The losers in this situation were the fans closest to the track that suddenly had their view obstructed by the skaters themselves.

Charlie O'Connell's biggest enemy, if one were to ask any fan at the time, was not Buddy Atkinson or Bert Wall, but the referee, who, it seemed, never failed to catch his slightest infractions, while missing obvious mischief from the other team. Certain actions required a dramatic answer, bringing the crowd to its feet with a gasp. If any of the Bomber girls were ever mistreated at any time by any male skater from the other team, Charlie O burst menacingly into the situation and the fans got ugly on the instant. Women-on-women mayhem was accepted, while violence (usually threatened) from men against women would provoke a near-riotous response, with O'Connell in the middle of it all. A game-losing bad call for the Bombers would prompt a profane loud rant in the infield, and more than once O'Connell had to be restrained lest he punch a referee, which he did on one shocking occasion. Totally annoyed with one of Ken Monte's teams in a televised match, he actually picked up a bench and brandished it so threateningly that the Bombers all ran for cover.

Charlie O'Connell appears here in a business suit while sidelined for an injury in 1962. Slacks, a golf sweater, and sunglasses would be his more casual attire in the 1970s when sidelined. Often injured, he was a personality to be reckoned with even with his arm in a sling.

Fans were regularly concerned with Charlie O'Connell's recovery from an injury at least once per series. A series in the Bay Area could last anywhere from one to four weeks with a single team.

Charlie O'Connell cared little for the women's game and would float the idea of an all-male sport wistfully to Jerry Seltzer on occasion. It took years for him to realize that the women were at least half the game's appeal for a large segment of the audience. He hated obvious theatrics and had a low opinion of the wilder approaches personality Ann Calvello would employ, like having green hair and anything that insulted the intelligence of the audience. Far into his career, his attitude toward it all softened considerably, and when the Derby was gone, he was almost affectionate, referring to Annis Jensen as "a real lady, a good ol' gal." Of the women who tried to revive the sport in the 1990s, specifically Ann and Joan Weston, he once said, "I think it's a shame. Give it a rest. Get out while you can still walk."

Charlie O'Connell's eventual skating partner, here in the late 1950s, is likely to be the second name to be called up in memory. Joan Weston, the smiling heroine of the Bay Bombers, was a helmet-throwing, tough-blocking all-star almost from her debut. A tall, beautiful, Southern California girl, her radiant smile sort of flew in the face of the maligned tough girl image. Even before she became a Bomber, while on visiting teams, she happily posed for pictures, signed their programs, and, significantly, talked sports.

Six

THE GOLDEN GIRL

Joan Weston, careening for the Chiefs in Oakland in 1963, did a good television interview, was photogenic (during this period the girls sometimes unaccountably courted a dour image), and had a realistic approach to the game. Like Charlie O'Connell, she was so much taller that she became quite accustomed to being the dominant focal point in any game she skated. She was a team captain early on, but the best was yet to come.

In Joan Weston, getting ready to dump the Bombers' Ann Bauer in a 1960s Oakland tilt, Jerry Seltzer had a company spokesperson who knew how to deal with the media. There was resentment toward her from fellow skaters since she often worked in the Derby front office and was seen by some as being too much of a company girl. During gripe sessions over potlucks at her apartment, she did not always agree with anything said of Selzer, who she said "was the best thing ever to happen to Roller Derby."

Joan Weston was a little more outgoing as a visiting skater, here challenging Annis Jensen (left) for supremacy. This is a rare image of Weston as a jammer in 1962. The pivot position (black helmet) was her usual place, controlling the pack at the front.

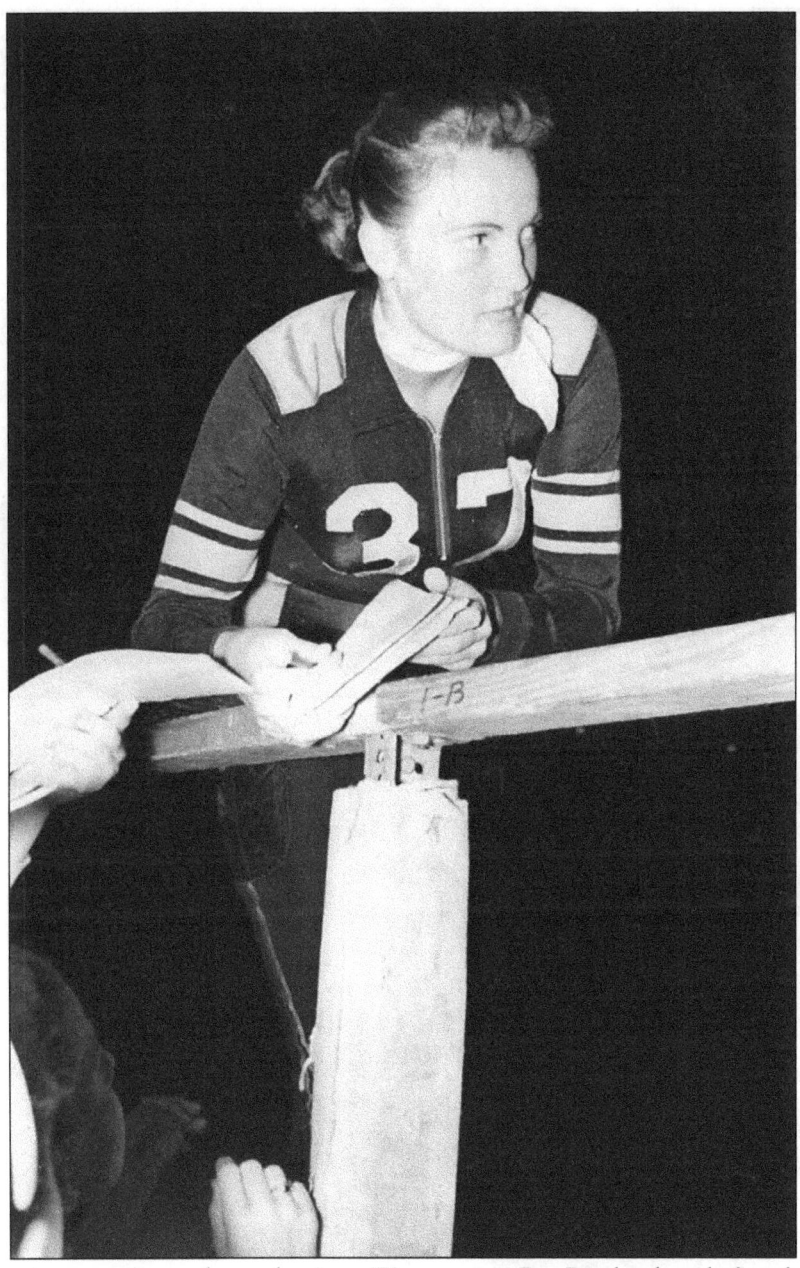

It will surprise many fans to learn that Joan Weston was a Bay Bomber long before she actually became women's captain of the team in 1965. Annis Jensen, fatefully, did not want to tour too far outside the Bay Area and certainly not on the endless cross-country tours the Bombers began in the 1960s. Bearing Jensen no resentment (she had paid her dues all over America since the 1940s for his father's company), Seltzer quietly slipped Weston into the Bomber leadership for low-profile road games and untelevised contests. Captaincy of the Bombers was seen as the ultimate career goal for a Roller Derby woman and resentment ran deep for Weston. Derby players often say she was "not a skater," that is, she could maneuver the track acceptably but without much proficiency. But she connected, she sold the game, and since it was not a completely genuine sport, this is what mattered most. She was also, as smitten reporters often would comment, a "really nice lady."

On the Chiefs, Joan Weston, No. 20, is about to send Annis Jensen into the rail. Through the years, other skaters have quietly remarked that these two liked to do everything themselves, and newer talent rarely got a chance to sparkle. The fans seemed not to notice, so long as "Big Red" or the "Blonde Amazon" was at the helm.

Three of the most popular personalities in the original game are seen jamming in the 1960s: Bomber scoring ace Judy Arnold (left) being chased by Joan Weston (center) with Annis Jensen at right. Within a couple of years, Jensen would be in semiretirement and Weston would be leading the Bombers with Arnold as her key backup.

Seven

THRILLS AND SPILLS

The Oakland Coliseum Arena opened in November 1966. The first three events were the miserable Oakland Seals playing NHL hockey. Roller Derby debuted the same week, and the Bombers drew more than 11,000 fans, surpassing the Seals for any game and setting an Oakland indoor sports attendance record. The local sports community was appalled.

Captain Joan Weston, No. 38, and Maureen O'Brien, No. 32, menace Joan Kazmerski, No. 21 of the Chiefs. Most of the league sported baseball script uniforms in the mid-1960s. Zippers divided the Bomber name on the Bombers' women's jersey.

Charlie O'Connell's Bay Bombers, with Joan Weston, No. 38, and "Peanuts," No. 34, are pictured here in 1965. Teams fielded five skaters at a time but usually had seven skaters on a squad for reserves. There are nine Bomber men because that was the way O'Connell wanted it. A number of young Bombers were placed on a kind of trial basis. Tony Roman (second row, fourth from left) would become a huge favorite. He would marry "Peanuts" that year and, per an honored custom, the two would forever share jersey No. 37. Along with Gil Orozco (second row, second from left) and Lou Donovan (second row, sixth from left), the most familiar faces to Bay Area Roller Derby fans included Tony Roman, Carol "Peanuts" Meyer, and Charlie O'Connell, all of whom skated in the Bombers last game in late 1973.

Charlie O' crosses the finish line first at a March of Dimes benefit Roller Derby game in Oakland. The Bombers raised hundreds of thousands of dollars for various causes in their day. Charity and Roller Derby go hand in hand, as present-day Bay Area Derby Girls are often involved in raising funds for causes like breast cancer research, aiding the homeless, domestic violence awareness, and more.

The newest Bomber, Joan Weston, battles the Texans' Darlene Anderson in 1965. Anderson is recognized as the first African American female in team sports. Since Annis Jensen was still so beloved by Bomber fans, Seltzer delayed her 1965 comeback with the Midwest Pioneers until late in Weston's first season, so Joan would have time to build up her fan base and the faithful would not be so torn to see their cherished "Big Red" going up against an interloper. Seltzer also decided to make her a cocaptain with the adored "Peanuts" Meyer, hoping Bomber fans would trust "Peanuts" with the team's fortunes while getting to know Weston.

Janet Earp, Joan Weston, Linda Murphy, Sue Fregulia, Dorothy Lee, Judy Arnold, Maureen O'Brien
Charlie O'Connell, Gil Orozco, Dave Battersby, Dewitte Quarles, Lou Donovan, Ronnie Jesus, Larry Smith

The 1966 Bombers are pictured here at the top of their game, in San Jose. Tony Roman had been drafted, "Peanuts" Meyer was gone, and Judy Arnold was Joan Weston's right-hand girl. Always somewhat in sync with the colors of the San Francisco Giants baseball team, the Bombers' colors were orange and deep brown, the patterns of which would vary wildly from season to season. Years later, Weston remarked with a laugh, "Whoever thought of orange and brown, I could kill 'em!"

San Francisco Bay Bombers

Janet Earp, Joan Weston, Carol Meyer, Dorothy Lee, Sue Fregulia, Sheila Peterson, Susan Jones, Maureen O'Brien
Gil Orozco, Charlie O'Connell, Tony Roman, Ron Kolsoozian, Bill Erghott, Julian Silva, Antoine Gilmore, Ernie Krueger

In the mid-1960s, "Charlie and I had finally gotten the game where we wanted it to be," commented Joan Weston years after the Derby had disappeared. The two of them were the stars, each had a key backup, a star jammer, and everything else was frosting on the cake. Antoine Gilmore (second row, second from right) was a Kenyan lion tamer and the skating Romans (No. 37) were back; otherwise, it was business as usual.

Bombers men ponder a huge crowd at the Oakland Coliseum Arena in 1966, snug in their new warm-up jackets. New uniforms were always exciting for the team, especially when this would happen in the middle of the season without warning, always a sign, Bomber Tony Roman once recalled fondly, of "how proud Jerry was of us and what the Derby was doing." Old uniforms were never thrown away. New uniforms were used for Sunday telecasts, while the previous season's outdated getup was used the rest of the week, away from the camera's eye. Uniforms had to be safe, photogenic, and last for years, becoming, with some alterations and patches, attire for other teams as long as they held out. They were so sturdy that, after the game ceased in 1973, would-be successor organizations doing "worked" games were using Roller Derby uniforms some 30 to 40 years after they were originally made. It was expensive and the design could have been kept the same, but *that*, Jerry Seltzer decreed, "would be dull."

Francine Cochu (right) and Joan Weston give a whip to "Peanuts" Meyer in 1969 at the Oakland Coliseum Arena. During the Bay Area season, getting a steady flow of fans to the same arena proved to be no easy task, hence, the Match Race. Taking its name from a 19th-century event where two horses of equal ability raced each other, the Derby adapted the concept to showcase young talent, or more profitably, to settle a beef between skaters, racing for 10 laps, then eight, then six. In chivalrous sexism, women raced for two laps less. Legal blocking was permitted, but sometimes, as Walt Harris grimly reported on the weekly broadcast, things "got out of hand" and illegal blocks, a scuffle, or a full-out fight occurred, halting the race. Nothing would do but to have the combatants try it again in San Jose or Richmond. Frequently, this would not settle the score; the unruly racers would "settle this once and for all, this Saturday night at the Cow Palace." Everyone was to call YUkon 2-7916 for reservations, and if the line was busy, Harris suggested, "Keep trying."

The 1970 World Championship Playoffs at the Cow Palace pits Charlie O'Connell against Roller Derby's "Blond Tiger" Jerry Cattell (right) of the Midwest Pioneers. Eddie Krebs (center, background) was a major jamming star who would briefly become Bombers coach a year later. National magazines, including *Time, Life,* the *New Yorker* and *Sports Illustrated,* all rediscovered the Derby between 1969 and 1970. Frank Deford, a young writer with *Sports Illustrated,* alarmed staid readers with a charming 15-page story on the Derby, which he expanded into the first book on the game, *Five Strides on the Banked Track.* A documentary film, *Derby,* was going to be a perfunctory look at the game and air on the syndicated television series, but filmmakers became so intrigued with the material and with a roustabout named Mike Snell from Ohio, who wanted to join the sport, that the film was split between track action, locker room kibitzing, and Snell's quest to play in the Derby. It stunned the film community's smart set and won ecstatic reviews, remaining on many critics' lists of all-time favorites for years to come.

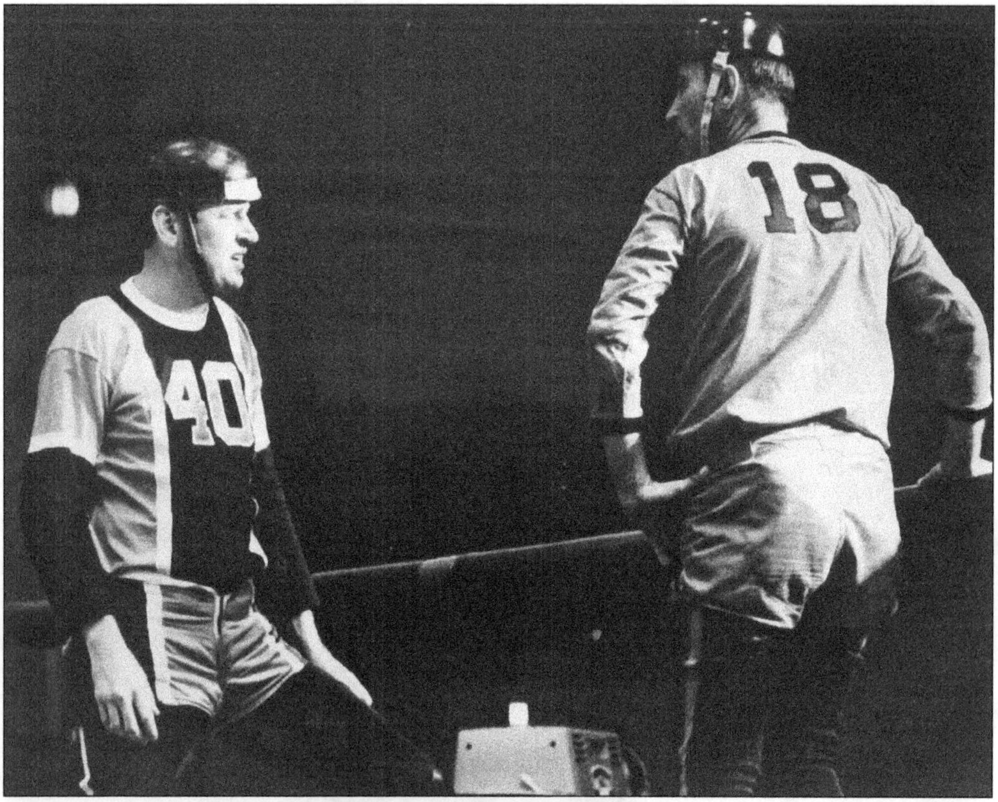

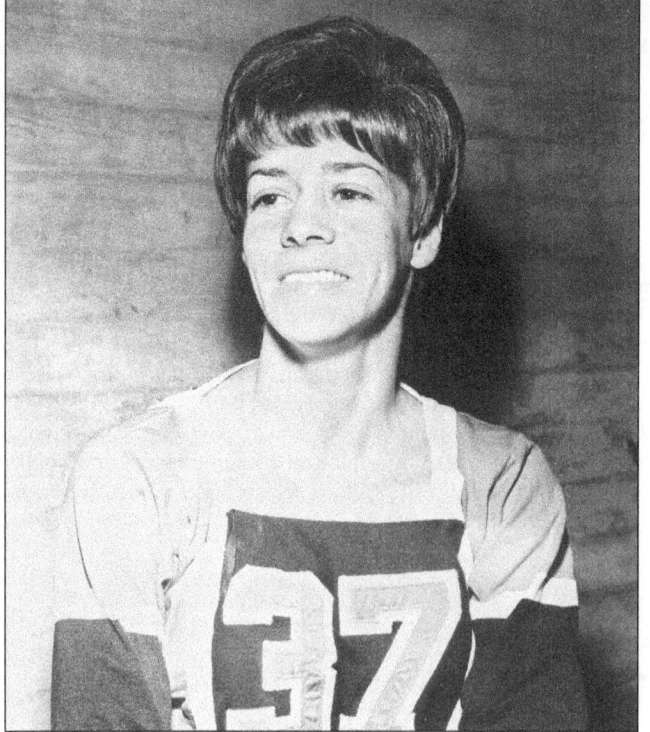

The warhorses, Bay Bombers' Charlie O'Connell (left) and Northwest Cardinal's Ken Monte, are in front of the cameras in 1969. Though they were hardly friends, per se, they appreciated each other's talent and similar approaches to the game.

"Peanuts" (Meyer) Roman, who twice was cocaptain of the Bombers, smiles for a portrait in 1969. "Peanuts" was a Bomber longer than any other skater except Charlie; it was said she was not that enamored of Joan Weston at first but learned to appreciate her appeal as the years rolled on.

The New England Braves' Ronnie Robinson, one of the game's most enduring stars, was a dynamic talent. Though a visitor, he was a Bay Area favorite and had memorable match races in 1968 and 1969 with Charlie O'Connell. A halftime interview Walt Harris would conduct during KTVU's live telecasts could result in a challenge from the visiting skater to his rival Bomber. If a Bomber issued a challenge, his or her opponent would accept on one condition: that his teammate could come along so that the Bomber could not pull any tricks. Sometimes another Bomber would be recruited for a two-person race; sometimes the race was two Braves or Chiefs against one Bomber. The Bombers would occasionally prevail, and uncertain outcomes kept ticket sales healthy. Anyone who stated that the Bombers would always win races or games was not a true fan; the Bombers lost . . . a lot. A record 21-game Bomber winning streak in 1972 was so alien that it has been all but forgotten. There was also a little Seltzerian strategy involved: if a skater lost a race, he hoped disappointed fans would rush for tickets to see him or the team emerge victorious the next time.

A rare photograph from 1968 shows the temporarily retired Charlie O'Connell looking like the relaxed infield coach he supposedly wanted to be. This was an almost totally new team for the Bay Area but would basically serve as their lineup until the end of the original game six years later. Cherished, loyal Bomber Gil Orozco, No. 39, was back again with Bob Woodbury, No. 38, now the men's team captain. Cliff Butler, No. 37, was a spectacular skater, then new to the team and adored by fans to the end. Larry Smith and Francine Cochu, No. 33, were the newest husband-and-wife team. Fresh from Canada, Cochu spoke little English when they started dating. Annis Jensen's daughter Barbara Baker, No. 39 (second row), was in her first season. Jensen was back skating with the Cardinals and could barely contain her enthusiasm when their teams met. "I've skated with my mother a few times; I've skated against her a few times," Baker recalled with a smile. "She broke my nose once . . . isn't she wonderful? She wanted her points!"

The 1969 Bombers are pictured here on a summer night in San Jose. Delores Tucker, No. 34, was Joan Weston's backup talent. "Big" Cal Stephens, No. 34, who never seemed to quite fit his uniform, was a rookie; in three years, he would be an emergency Bomber coach. These paneled uniforms, brown undershirt optional, are among the fans' favorites. Skaters had some elbow and knee padding but not much. The only padding everyone wore was usually a thin, foam "butt pad," which made the nightly crashing to the track more bearable (and even added some bounce).

The 1968 Bombers meet the Northwest Cardinals in "the only game of the year in Vallejo." Many cities got one or two chances a year to prove they were loyal. Today, several of these communities have their own Derby team. Regular stops included Gilroy (represented today by the South County Derby Girls), Antioch (the Undead Bettys League), Eureka (Humbolt Roller Derby), Fresno (SINtral Valley Derby Girls), and Ukiah (Deep Valley Belligerents and the Mendo Mayhem Roller Girls).

Susie Wong, Candy Jones, Francine Cochu, Delores Tucker, Carolyn Moreland, Carol Meyer, Joan Weston, Barbara Baker
Alvin Mallory, Bobby Jennings, Larry Smith, Jim Jackson, Cliff Butler, Tony Roman, Gil Orozco, Charlie O'Connell

The Bombers are pictured here in 1971, Joan Weston's last season with the club. Big plans were afoot to break up the team by sending its most popular skaters to other clubs to establish three genuine home teams across the country.

DISTAFF WHEELERS -- The Chiefs' rugged distaff captain, Sandy Dunn (L), wheels against veteran Bomber Cathie Read (R). Read has placed on the All Star roster nine times in her 12 year career, while Dunn was the league's 1969 M.V.P. and rates seven consecutive All Star appearances. Both teams wheel in local action as part of the International Roller Derby League's 120-game 1971-72 season.

This photograph purports to showcase a New York–San Francisco matchup between the Chiefs' Sandy Dunn (left) and Cathie Read (No. 37) of the hometown Bombers, but it is a posed (for photographers) "game" at an empty Kezar Pavilion in 1971, one of many sent out to newspapers to herald a new look that, incredibly, would signal the end of the game nearly two years later.

Bay Area girls Barbara Baker (left) and Carolyn Moreland warm up for Madison Square Garden's Chiefs club in the 1970s. The Chiefs had disappeared from Derby for three years. The team was unique in that it was one of the few times outsiders had any financial piece of any team. Charlie O'Connell was named the new coach, stunning Bay Area fans.

Sellout crowds for the Bay Bombers at Madison Square Garden occurring repeatedly, guaranteeing New Yorkers their own team in 1971.

The notorious Ann Calvello in 1973 is rolling for the Red Devils at Kezar. In a few weeks, a match race gone wrong will result in Bob Woodbury accidentally crashing onto her leg, keeping her from skating to the end of the original Derby. She had developed quite a rivalry in the late 1960s with Joan Weston, on track and off. Always happily associated with Roller Derby and something of an expert at self-promotion, Calvello was affiliated with innumerable skating units and promotions after Roller Derby ended, eventually becoming the subject of a lovingly quirky film documentary, *Demon of the Derby*, in 2001. Her frank comments did not always endear her to her fellow skaters, and she was something of a loner among Derby women. Toward the end of her life, she was touched when contemporary roller girls would hail her as an inspiration and a pioneer for women in sports, and her loyal network of fans was in constant contact. She passed away in 2006.

Joan Weston and the Pioneers skate before a record crowd of more than 50,000 at White Sox Park in the fall of 1972; incredibly, Roller Derby would be out of business a little more than a year later.

Delores Tucker (right), here attempting to give the heave-ho to Carolyn Maryland, became the Bombers women's captain after Joan left for the Midwest Pioneers. She was a solid fan favorite, yet in the Bombers' final season, "Peanuts" Meyer and Margie Laszlo were named cocaptains.

The Bombers are on tour at the Chicago Amphitheater in 1971. For sentimental reasons, Seltzer scheduled Bomber touring games at the crumbling Chicago Coliseum in the 1960s, long past the venue's usefulness. Convinced that the building was increasingly unsafe, he began scheduling games at the newer Chicago Amphitheater when the Bay Bombers were on tour in the area. Skaters proudly recall Seltzer always tried to make Derby the first event in any new venue.

A number of skaters became major stars when the Derby expanded to a home-team format in 1971. The Pioneers' Darlene Forbes (left) became Joan's "second skater" on the Pioneers, to the delight of Midwest fans. The Cincinnati Jolters had the talents of Francine Cochu, a Bay Area favorite. It was somewhat illusionary; home teams or not, the entire International Roller Derby League lived in the Bay Area.

Kathy Pulliam, Debbie Cho, Delores Tucker, Linda Antonio, Armeda Ortiz, Carol Meyer, Marge Laszlo
Alvin Mallory, James Paul, Bob Dancel, Pete Boyd, Tony Roman, Jim Cook, Gil Orozco, Charlie O'Connell

This is the final lineup for Roller Derby's Bay Bombers in 1973. Veteran skaters were a little on the shy side about having their picture taken (notable exception was former model Margie Laszlo), but new skaters livened up the photograph and, Seltzer hoped, the game itself. Attendance was plummeting, however, and no one could pinpoint why.

Jerry Cattell (left) and Bill Grill put the squeeze on Tony Roman in a posed 1971 photo session at the Derby's training school in Alameda, an old automotive garage. Note the broken line on the track indicating the path trainees should take to negotiate the five stride that took them in and out of turns.

103

In the 1970 playoffs in San Francisco, the Cardinals' Mike Gammon (left) battles Eddie Krebs of the Pioneers. Visiting teams skated often at Bay Area venues. For the 1970 and 1971 cross-country tour, the Bombers split into two. There were the Oakland Bay Bombers, with Joan Weston and Ken Monte playing the Braves, and Charlie O'Connell and the San Francisco Bay Bombers. And Margie Laszlo was in Joan Weston's role, chasing the Pioneers. This doubled the scope of the tour. The original Roller Derby's zenith is considered to be 1971. Bomber attendance in the Bay Area was dependable and ratings were healthy, in some cases spectacular on the Derby's 110-station syndicated network. In the fall, Charlie O'Connell was injured, and, unusually, Joan Weston was out of action too. Buddy Atkinson Jr. was coaxed from semiretirement to lead the Bombers into the playoffs, while Lydia Clay was at the helm of the girls' squad. Walt Harris warned viewers of big expansion and a player draft with each team able to protect only three skaters. Fans assumed that two Bombers safe from being drafted would be Charlie and Joan, but they were wrong.

A publicity photographer captured the mood of the July 4, 1971, Derby event at the Oakland Coliseum where the Bombers' record attendance of more than 34,000 fans was set. Fans were encouraged to wave their plastic flags on cue during a fireworks presentation. At upper right, Jerry Seltzer observes his father's creation. Two weeks after the Bombers won the championship that fall, the club was part of what would be an eventual six-team circuit, including the Central Pioneers (with Joan Weston, Gil Orozco, Tony Roman, and "Peanuts" Meyer) representing Chicago, the Midwest Jolters (with Cliff Butler, Ann Calvello and Margie Laszlo), and the Northeast Chiefs (with Charlie, the main Bomber, set to coach). The Bomber stars were dispersed among the needy. The Red Devils, Eagles, and suddenly nondescript Bombers, who had a series of coaches and Delores Tucker as the women's captain, were the visiting teams. In January 1972, to the amazement of all and the heartbreak of the Bay Area fans, Walt Harris himself announced on KTVU news that the Bombers had been sold to Texas investors who wanted to move America's only regional sports team to the Southwest.

In the pre-Internet days, Bomber fans watched reruns of their team in 1972 and hoped for the best, not realizing "Peanuts" Meyer (left) and Francine Cochu were off the orange and brown.

Charlie O'Connell was honored as Bomber coach in the fall of 1971 with a special playoff program as he announced he was indeed coaching the new Chiefs team out of Madison Square Garden. Bay Area fans, they learned next spring, acted like typical fans of legitimate sports, considering this a total betrayal.

A rare shot of fans' favorite visiting team uniforms as Jan Vallow, bashing the Bombers' Delores Tucker, models the look of the Southern Mustangs. Vallow was rookie of the year in 1959 with the Bombers; some of her successive fame took place in a competing outfit, but she returned to the true Derby in 1970 with her husband, Nick Scopas. Eventually, they skated for the Braves. Though they battled ferociously on the track, Vallow was close friends with Joan Weston in reality. Seemingly vicious, she was vilified by fans to such a degree that when her team would play Ann Calvello's, the fans almost invariably got behind Calvello's squad. Off track, she was among the most revered skaters of all, gentle, kind, and concerned about the dignity and professionalism of the skaters and the game itself. She often volunteered her time to work with new talent in would-be successor leagues and was, like Weston, a mother hen to her team; her skaters idolized her. Always ready to help, she proudly served the Bombers on tour on more than one occasion.

Jerry Cattell is dumped by the Bombers in this photograph, which purports to be a still from the movie *Derby* but is in reality just a shot from a typical game. Jerry Seltzer never intended to give up the Bay Area. Devastated followers were promised that Charlie O'Connell's Chiefs would play a summer season in the Bay Area. Tongue firmly in cheek, with an eye on the absurdity of sports teams ashamed to be playing in troubled Oakland and being called "Golden" instead, Seltzer told the press that the Chiefs official name would be the California Golden Golden State Bay Area Chiefs, seemingly serious about the two "Goldens." Bay Area Chiefs openers were well attended by dejected fans who booed O'Connell and sometimes cheered the opposing team (Bob Woodbury's Red Devils). The situation was even more stark two weeks after the season started when Joan Weston's Pioneers came to town and were in many venues celebrated as the home team. All was well that ended reasonably well; the Bombers came back after insufficient financing voided their sale.

"It was a tough time for the fans," Joan Weston recalled of the era she skated for the Midwest Pioneers. "They were really torn." It was common for audiences to root against the Bombers when the Pioneers were in town; even more surreal would be situations where the crowd would root for the Pioneer women and the Bomber men, or individual skaters on jams. Most of the Bomber stars came back except for Joan Weston, who was asked by Seltzer to stay on with the Pioneers. She was a tremendous draw, but the Bombers never again had the kind of box office certainty at home when the "Blonde Amazon" was on the team. The year 1972 seemed to be a giddy time for the game. Seltzer held a press conference to introduce "Mama" Cass Elliot to the press for a planned movie, *Jam*, about Derby life. The Pioneers and Chiefs filled up hinterland dates in Northern California locales like Ukiah and Antioch. The DeYoung Museum requested a Bay Bomber helmet for a display, causing Seltzer to note that now Roller Derby qualified as an art form. However, after a player strike that fall and a disastrous touring season, the jam would suddenly end before everyone could even grasp what was happening.

Joan Weston was in the final series at Kezar Pavilion in 1973, dropping the Bombers' Debbie Cho in the now ubiquitous birdcage gear.

Eddie Krebs was the penultimate Bomber coach before the team returned to the Bay Area. A melancholy presence in the *Derby* film, he was on something of a comeback when he suffered a career-ending injury on the road.

Joan Weston is pictured here in her final Roller Derby role on the Midwest Pioneers. She would have preferred to return to the Bombers but wanted to do what was best for the game. Her popularity was such that the Pioneers became the moneymaking team for the last two years of the original Derby. "I won't be around forever," she once remarked, "but I'd like to always know Roller Derby will be."

When skaters like Judi McGuire (left) and Pearl Quilici assembled for photographs at Kezar Pavilion in their brand new uniforms in the fall of 1971, it was thought that it was the beginning of the best times for Roller Derby. "We realized later," Jerry Seltzer recalled, "that it was really the beginning of the end."

Mike Gammon takes a breather in the troubled final season of Roller Derby. "There was a lot of complaining about stuff in the last couple years," he recalled in 1999, "and when times got tough, people said they'd skate for free 'til things got better. But it was too late for that. It was past that." The embarrassing 1972 strike lasted only two days, yet hard feelings among some lasted for decades. The local press was so shocked that the incident was buried in small, unnoticeable stories in the back of the newspapers. The spectacle of 50 picketing skaters rolling around the Kaiser Center in Oakland was somewhat pathetic, and skater demands, like a 40-week season and a minuscule salary, was rather humiliating for all concerned. Recalling Jerry Seltzer, Tony Roman remarked poignantly, "I have my family because of his family. He didn't deserve that." Joan Weston was just as succinct in her feelings. "That whole affair broke his heart," she once recalled. "He was never the same after that."

Judi McGuire (left) and Carolyn Maryland (center) have a tense talk with Joan Weston in the final Roller Derby game on Long Island, on December 8, 1973. Dwindling attendance, inflation, the gas shortage, legal issues with a former investor, and a multitude of other problems led to the end of the game as it had been known for almost 40 years.

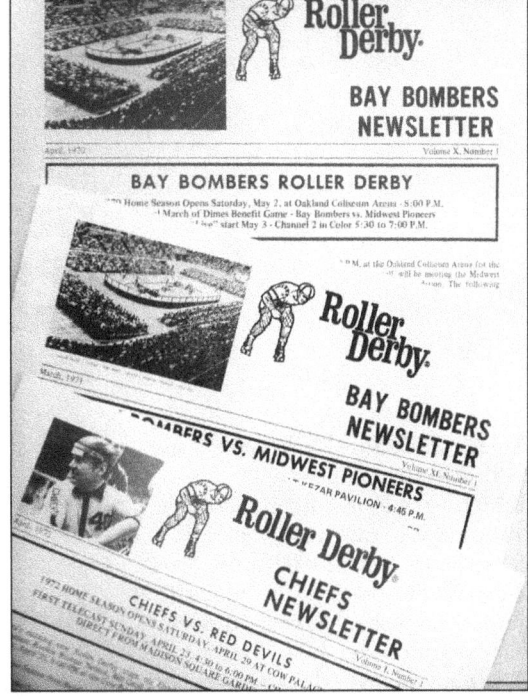

Throughout the 1960s, Bay Area fans on the Bay Bomber mailing list eagerly awaited newsletters telling of upcoming games in their area or information on when the Bombers would return.

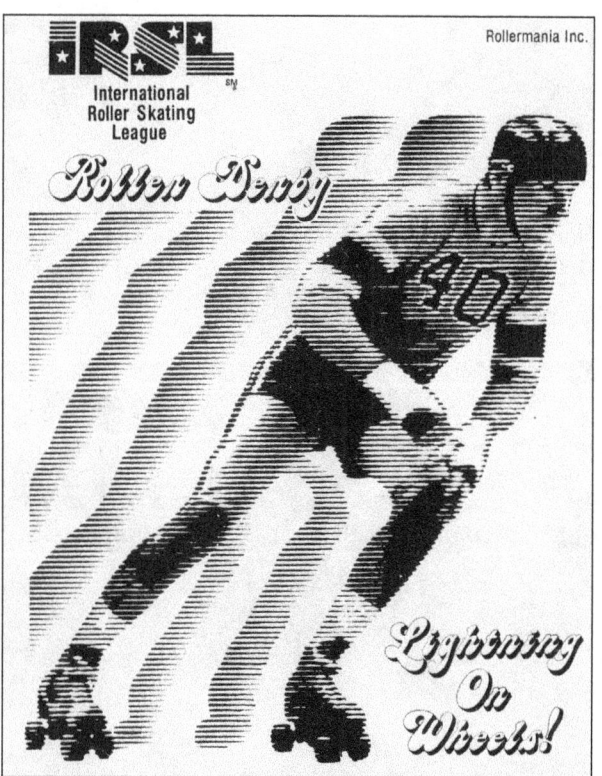

The International Roller Skating League made a decade-long effort to revive the game in the Bay Area. Though it showed promise, it faded out in the 1980s, in part because of the aging of the Seltzer-era skaters and the inability to attract new faces to the game.

American Skating Derby took skaters willing to volunteer for a set of games at high schools and other charitable institutions to raise money for local causes, including Morale at the Naval Weapons Station in Concord. Little money was made, but veteran talent like Barbara Baker, Joan Weston, and Ann Calvello gave their best shot.

Eight

BEYOND THE BOMBERS

Fans and skaters of the long-gone game were heartbroken at Joan Weston's death at 62 from Creutzfeldt–Jakob disease in 1997. Delores Tucker remarked at her passing, "She was kind of the mother of us all." An appreciation of her life and the defunct game in the *New York Times* sparked interest and memories, eventually inspiring a slick television reboot called *Rollerjam*.

Although *Rollerjam* had sensational skaters, inline wheels for the 1990s, and eye-catching young talent, it never sparked enough interest in a live event. Scriptwriters, and an approach too close to wrestling, doomed the concept to appeal mainly to kids and few others. In a portent of things to come, the tough-talking New York Enforcers (left), a "visiting" team, became the most popular squad.

A long way from Kezar Pavilion, *Rollerjam*'s "Bod Squad," chats up Jay Leno. From left to right are Cindy Zimmermann, Jamie Conemac, and Stacey Blistch. The ladies were great skaters and enthusiastic personalities. Many *Rollerjam* players have joined different skating ventures. Blistch in particular looks for ways to use her talents and communication skills to promote positive images and healthy choices for young people. (Courtesy of "Malibu" Stacey Blistch.)

Roller Derby's Hall of Fame, dormant since 1973, was revived by Brooklyn fan Gary Powers in the 1990s with the startled blessing of Jerry Seltzer. Joan Weston and others that did not have a chance to be honored as members have been celebrated through the years, and Gary's devotion to the original game, its offshoots, and its skaters have surprised many. Fallen on hard times, skaters have received a helping hand from Gary Powers and a special group of Derby fans.

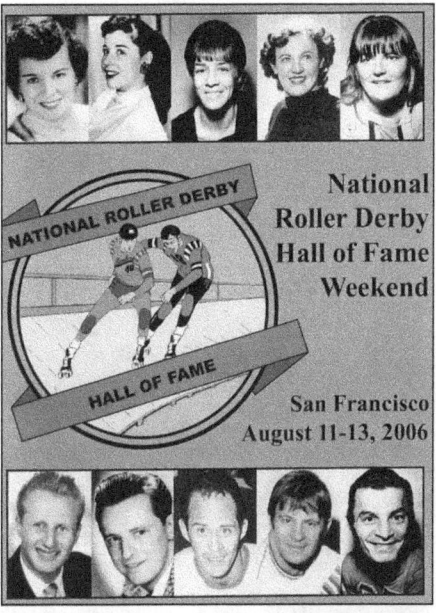

In the 21st-century world of the Bay Area roller girls, the Richmond Wrecking Belles host the Berkeley Resistance just a few blocks away from where the beloved Bay Bombers took on their opponents at the Richmond Auditorium. This time, however, it is all real. Prior to a typical bout, skaters are everywhere, exchanging jokes and worried looks, posing for pictures, talking team strategy—attractive ladies in absurd but safe outfits. The best seats are those on the floor right next to the action.

At a roller girl event, families and friends get as close to the action as possible.

The Richmond Wrecking Crew has a strategy session before their bout. Though players' skate names (such as Cheap Trixie, Genghis Mom, and Katie Karnage) bring smiles and laughter, the game itself is untouchably sport.

La Lucha, of the Sac City Rollers League (her team is the Capital Punishers), greets fans in a 2012 bout. A competitor since 2005 ("Broke my ankle and have the screws and plates to prove it"), she offers a typical breezy comment on why she remains with the game: the Derby "saved my life!" Like his father, Jerry Seltzer is somewhat concerned that theatrical, tongue-in-cheek "track" names do not make it easy for the sport to gain acceptance in the athletic world but also points out "they have to be individuals before they can be a team." (Courtesy Donalee Eiri.)

The Chiefs' Sandy Dunn (left) gives it her all against San Francisco's Margie Laszlo in their last matchup in New York before the Derby halted its league just weeks later. A lot of veteran talent attempted to revive the game, as they knew it, and looked with bemusement at female-only leagues skating legitimately in the 21st century. They later began to take it seriously.

The Sac City Rollers are pictured in action (above), and the "Lipstick Librarian" limbers up (below). At present, scores of leagues exist in the United States and beyond. It is apparent that funding is required for all of the leagues, and although some can make it on their own now because of the ability to draw sufficient crowds in their facilities to bear some of the league costs, they represent a minuscule amount of the total leagues. And there is a catch-22: to move to the large arenas and to promote the matches sufficient enough to get a large crowd requires a large amount of money, something never in huge supply for Roller Derby. (Courtesy of Donalee Eiri.)

In some ways, the current game is a paradox. It is pure sport played with entertaining elements (the team names; the *nom de skate* each player creates, preventing her from being recognized for the superb athlete she often is; and so on), as opposed to the original attraction, which was something of an imitation of sport. While frivolous, fun, and enjoyable, some worry that the entertaining aspects prevent mass acceptance of the new game. Others point out that mass acceptance was never the issue, that Roller Derby, in any form, is something to enjoy. In some ways, the current game is a send-up of the original, except that it is real. (Above, courtesy of Donalee Eiri; below, courtesy of Windy Welch.)

In 2011, Jerry Seltzer reunited with early Bay Bomber star Judy Sowinksi, coaching her Penn Jersey Devils. Seltzer was impressed with the skaters' dedication and skill and even more so with Judy's tireless coaching at age 70.

The future of the game in the Bay Area and beyond has always been its youngest participants. Here, "Lil Trouble" and "Princess Die" celebrate a win for their Silicon Valley Roller Girls junior Derby team. (Courtesy of Taira Price.)

A number of the women's leagues that have appeared virtually overnight have participants that avoid body contact as they learn to negotiate the game, but the Sac City Roller Girls have no such qualms about mixing it up. Lipstick Librarian (second from left) and the ladies battle for position in 2011. (Courtesy Donalee Eiri.)

Skaters still in action when the original game ended in 1973, particularly those who have tried to restart it with all manner of doomed revivals since then, were at first reluctant to embrace the new, legitimate incarnation of the sport, though expressing admiration for the new game's talent. Players from the earliest days of the sport, those that competed in Leo Seltzer's era ending in the 1950s, however, have been more supportive, not surprisingly since their tenures featured less theatrics than in successive years. With the contemporary celebration of the game and films like *Derby Baby* occurring more and more, veteran Derby personnel have come around, especially now that men's leagues are beginning to catch on. Some skaters have reappeared as coaches, advisors, and fans. Here, Bay Bomber star Cliff Butler proudly joins an assembly of new talent in 2010.

Pictured here is the classic roller girl; the future of the game looks limitless.

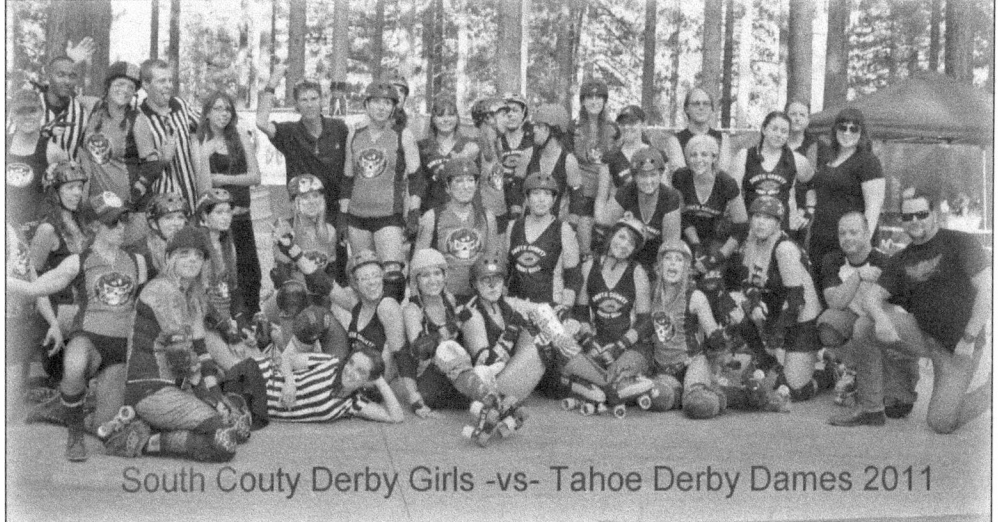

South Couty Derby Girls -vs- Tahoe Derby Dames 2011

Gilroy was another of the Bombers' annual stops. In 2011, the South City Rollergirls of Gilroy proudly assemble under the redwoods for their very first bout against the Tahoe Derby Dames. (Courtesy of Der-T-Dexter.)

Every venue is different, the Tahoe Derby Dames just happen to have one of the most beautiful bout locales. (Courtesy of Der-T-Dexter.)

While keeping an eye on the new, superfan Gary Powers collects artifacts from the original game, which he displays in his Brooklyn home.

This photograph by Rich Filice depicts the amazingly strong circle of trust, friendship, and love that these women all have for one another, which seems to be so prevalent in Roller Derby. The meaning behind this image was eternalized by the horrible loss of one of the Derby girls to domestic violence, which led to the addition of the purple ribbon. Lynn Shimek (in the upper right of the circle with striped socks and ribbon in her hair) was the tragic victim. "In Roller Derby," Ann Calvello once noted, "the name of the game is teamwork. We gotta always stand together." (Courtesy of Rich Filice.)

Visit us at
arcadiapublishing.com